Praise for *Think Like a Marketer*

Practical wisdom and pragmatic advice for anyone who wants to grow their business. This is loaded with proven ideas and dynamic strategies that can benefit everyone.

—Dr. Nido R. Quebin, president,
High Point University, High Point, NC

Effective marketing requires a dogged mindset, and Think Like a Marketer *shares key strategies for doing this instinctively and systematically. Entrepreneurs who want to grow and succeed in today's challenging and competitive economy need to read this book!*

—Karen Kerrigan, president and CEO,
Small Business and Entrepreneurship Council and
founder, Women Entrepreneurs, Inc.

Lauron's four secrets to standing out say it so simply—yet significantly. They are the signature story of marketing success, no matter the industry or the product.

—Dianna Booher, author of *The Voice of Authority* and
Booher's Rules of Business Grammar

Lauron was instrumental in getting my online business launched in 1996. Today, that start-up is worth several millions of dollars. Anyone looking to get to that top spot needs to read this book!

—Dr. Dhavid Cooper, CEO, FramesDirect.com

Think Like a Marketer *is the small business owner's dream manual. Lauron provides a clear and concise action plan to put you on the path to easy and automatic marketing success.*

—Al Lautenslager,
author of *Guerrilla Marketing In 30 Days*

With the flair of her spirited Cajun heritage, Sonnier gets down to the details of how to turn the many assets of an organization into a rich, blended stew of marketing opportunity that keeps a company growing and thriving.

—Sandy Lawrence, president, Perceptive Marketing,
Houston, TX

Lauron Sonnier

Think Like a Marketer

What It Really Takes to Stand Out From the Crowd, the Clutter, and the Competition

CAREER
PRESS
Franklin Lakes, NJ

THINK LIKE A MARKETER
EDITED BY KATE HENCHES
TYPESET BY EILEEN MUNSON
Cover design by Eric Ottinger, O Positive Design
Printed in the U.S.A.

To order this title, please call toll-free 1-800-CAREER-1 (NJ and Canada: 201-848-0310) to order using VISA or MasterCard, or for further information on books from Career Press.

The Career Press, Inc., 3 Tice Road, PO Box 687,
Franklin Lakes, NJ 07417
www.careerpress.com

Library of Congress Cataloging-in-Publication Data
Sonnier, Lauron.
     Think like a marketer : what it really takes to stand out from the crowd, the clutter, and the competition / by Lauron Sonnier.
          p. cm.
     Includes index.
     ISBN 978-1-60163-073-5
          1. Marketing. 2. Marketing—Management. I. Title.

HF5415.S6933 2009
658.8--dc22

                                                                              2009007767

To Madeline and Sarah:
You stir the greatest of emotions in me.
You need no marketing, ever.

Acknowledgments

I have long thought it odd that books included acknowledgments. Twice I have gone through childbirth, which I would consider to be the grandest of feats, and yet, even for that, there is no customary rite of certification. No one expected me to place a notice in the local newspaper to formally thank my gynecologist, nurses, husband, the people who were fortunately present when I went into labor, and the barista at Starbucks who knew what I wanted every morning as I hit the drive-through.

Now that I have actually completed the writing and publishing process, I realize that the baby thing might be trumped after all. I have come to understand the necessity of the acknowledgments page, and I am delighted to memorialize my gratitude for the many who have assisted me during this book's pregnancy and labor.

Actually, it's very empowering. It's like being nominated for an Oscar and writing your acceptance speech in case you need it, only you absolutely get to use it. And instead of a few fleeting seconds of quickly-forgotten fame on national television, you get to apply the power of print to chisel a permanent message of thanks to all who hold a particularly special place in your belly.

So here goes. I proudly acknowledge and send my deepest gratitude to the academy of supporters who made this book possible.

To my agent, John Willig, who championed the idea full throttle. John is the real deal as an agent, literary man, and human. Plus, he comes with a bucketful of encouragement, and every writer needs that.

To the talented people of Career Press who get things done and make things happen. Thank you for helping me achieve something meaningful and for making the process so easy.

To my husband, Marc Stewart, for your undying support in every way and for wittingly occupying two children so I could accomplish what I have always been destined to do.

To Jim Serra of KPLC-TV in Lake Charles, Louisiana, for giving a young pup a big chance and for being such a valued friend and contributor to my evolution as an enlightened and successful being.

To Randy Rasch and Brandon Rasch for paving the way for me to jump into the sharky waters of marketing. Thank you for throwing me a lifeline and helping me go out on my own as a true marketing professional. I am forever grateful to you for believing in me and giving me the shot of a lifetime to become a struggling entrepreneur.

To Dr. Dhavid Cooper for your gentle nudging and terrific encouragement. Thank you for awakening me to the real power of possibility.

To Valerie Boudreaux-Allen who has been one of my greatest inspirations and sources of comfort in business and life. You are such an extraordinary gift, and I could never thank you enough. Your path to Heaven is well paved for all you have done for me alone.

To my assistant, Zoe Russell, for your eagle eye and ever-diligent support. You are enormously appreciated, and your impact is far greater than you know.

To the many wonderful companies and business owners who have chosen me to assist them. Thank you for your confidence and for helping me build my business while I helped you build yours. I appreciate you all.

To my mother, Elsie Darnell Sonnier, a woman of great character, tremendous talent, and utter selflessness who taught me how to "stir the pot." You are immensely loved and sorely missed. We'll never eat so well without you.

Finally, to Paul McCulloch, who always believed I could and would do this, and who I know drops me bits of comedy and wisdom from the Heavens.

Thank you all for being angels in my life. I am honored to share your goodness and well-taught wisdom in these pages.

Contents

. ■ .

Introduction

Time to get clear and confident

Peple make marketing far too complicated. They get stuck in cumbersome strategies, follow the crowd without knowing where it's going, and believe they have to spend a lot of money to make marketing work.

The problem is that they aren't thinking like marketers. In fact, they may not be thinking at all. When it comes to marketing, I believe most business owners and managers are working much harder than they have to. Maybe you are, too.

Most are missing hundreds of marketing opportunities that stare them in the face in the everyday operation of their business. Maybe you are, too.

Most are wasting time, money, and optimism on haphazard marketing efforts, only to get minimal returns and diminish all faith in the very thing that can help them excel. Maybe you are, too.

If this is you, or ever has been you, then it's time to re-think marketing.

This book is about making marketing practical, easy, even automatic. It's about showing you a new way to think and approach your business so marketing gets done and gets results.

As a small business owner, I understand firsthand the challenges marketing can pose, especially for a small or mid-size enterprise. I also understand the consequences that come from neglecting it. If you want to be successful, marketing is not an option. But then, why wouldn't you be anxious and thrilled to market your business and yourself? You chose to do what you do. I'm assuming you offer a product or service that can benefit others. Why wouldn't you be ecstatic to tell the world about it?

I know it's not always easy, and I know all of the excuses—the list of "not enough's." Not enough time. Not enough money. Not enough people. Not enough expertise. Well, enough with all that. It's time to get out of your own way. It's time to make marketing doable and, most importantly, integrated into the day-to-day running of your business, so it happens in spite of yourself and even while you're chasing fires.

It's time to stir things up.

If you are one of the "most" who have found marketing to be confusing and overwhelming, take heart and take a deep breath. Your world is about to get much easier. I will demystify marketing so you can act with a level head and fresh perspective on the marketing opportunities that abound right under your nose. You'll learn how to stand out from the crowd and the clutter. You'll learn how to outperform the competition by outthinking the competition. And, you'll learn how to transform your business into a marketing machine. What is mind-boggling and frustrating about marketing today will become easy, natural, and business-as-usual tomorrow. In fact, I'm confident that, with your new marketing mindset, you'll change how you do business forever.

Marketing does not have to be complicated, and you can make big things happen in your business even with your limited resources. I know because I've done it for my customers and my own business. I have dedicated my entire career to helping small, but aggressive businesses reach their marketing potential while doing the best with what they had.

My favorite personal success story involves a mature, business-to-business company of 23 years. It had reached about $1 million in sales. It was successful by all accounts in its industry and marketplace, but wanted to take the next leap. Traditional sales efforts weren't working well enough. The company needed to reach deeper and wider. So, we created a program that integrated marketing into the day-to-day operation of the business. We worked and kneaded it until marketing became as natural and as common as making payroll and paying taxes. We sniffed and sought out every opportunity to get a meaningful message to the target audience consistently and constantly. By thinking like a marketer, we had the guidance we needed to capitalize on opportunities that would be completely unrecognizable to the average company. In four years, sales doubled to more than $2.1 million with notably no major operational changes, a bare-bones budget, and, get this, not one outside salesperson. This is living proof that, when you think like a marketer, you can make magical things happen in your business, even with all of those "not enough's."

Now it's your turn to get a mental marketing adjustment. If you have struggled in making marketing happen and misfired in making it effective, things are about to change. We are about to drill down to the very essence of what marketing really is and what it means for you every day in the normal running of your business. We'll explore the timeless principles that transcend the latest trends and technological exploits. And, I'll teach you how to put marketing into action and how to keep it there—so you'll have a great success story, too. The best part is that you will know exactly what to do when you shut the book.

As you read, make notes, highlight passages, dog-ear pages, and really ponder the questions posed. This book is packed with principles to guide you, questions to challenge you, and tips and tools to help you put your newfound learning into practice.

The time has come to get clear and confident in your marketing, so grab your pen and open your mind. Get ready to think like a marketer. Get ready to stand out from the crowd, the clutter, and the competition. Get ready to be a marketing machine!

ARE YOU READY

to think like a marketer?

ARE YOU READY

to stand out from the crowd, the clutter, and the competition?

ARE YOU READY

to be a marketing machine?

■

*You can do it,
and it's easier than you think.*

Be prepared to change how you do business forever.

PHASE 1

Getting Into a Marketing Mindset

Everything is marketing.

Chapter I

Inside the Marketer's Head

A *different way of thinking*

To think like a marketer, you must first understand how a marketer thinks, so let's peer into the mind of this distinctive breed of creative and analytical types, and combinations thereof.

Marketers run through life with their minds wide open. They operate from a big-picture perspective while still keeping their eyes on the finest details. They are optimists, always seeing the glass as half-full even when it is completely empty. They see opportunities everywhere and they strive never to leave anything on the table.

Marketers are bold in thought and swift in action. They move with urgency, pouncing on every good chance knowing it could be gone in a click. They aren't afraid to make the call, ask the imposing question, and "go there" when necessary. Marketers are confident, persistent, and fully dedicated to their cause no matter where it takes them.

Marketers become smart people readers because they are avid people watchers. They are curious, anxious to see what's happening, and what's happening next. Their unquenchable thirst for understanding, and sometimes a little nosiness, puts them often in the right place at the right time— sometimes by strategy and sometimes by luck, though luck is always part of the strategy.

Marketers ask questions—lots and lots of questions. They turn the tables to peer in from the other's perspective, understanding that it is the "other" who makes their job interesting, rewarding, and necessary.

Marketers live and operate on the fringe. They are weird, odd, off-center, out there, and generally different from the rest. To them, conformity is to be avoided at all costs. They love to stand out and they will do anything for attention, as long as it's the right kind of attention.

On the down side, marketers must be wary of overload and incompletion, for they are always anxious for the next pursuit and quickly bored with the one at hand. They must work to focus their minds, albeit difficult with so many great ideas swirling about their brains. Still, marketers must organize their time and concentrate their attention wisely, or they'll be overly stretched and overly busy without seeing anything finished.

Above all, marketers are thinkers—big thinkers, deep thinkers, pervasive thinkers. They are always wondering what if, how could, and why not. They see possibility when others see nothing, and they aren't easily put off by naysayers, non-believers, or risk.

Marketers are rainmakers and difference-makers. They take charge, working strategically and mindfully to do whatever it rightfully takes to achieve their goals. They are constantly stirring things up, and they make good things happen for the companies they represent, the people they employ, and the universe they serve.

The marketer is a unique breed indeed, and certainly not a role for the faint of will. But then, neither is that of entrepreneur, business owner, or manager. If you can conquer those fates, then surely you can handle a little marketing. One thing is for certain—your business needs it. You owe it to yourself, your business, and your marketplace to be a smart and aggressive marketer. It's easier than you think, as long as you think like a marketer.

Chapter 2

What Smart Marketers Know

Think like a marketer and you'll act like a marketer. Act like a marketer and magical things will happen in your business.

Most people have a slippery understanding of what marketing really is, including many people charged with doing it. If your idea of marketing is inaccurate or incomplete, then you are vulnerable to costly mistakes, lost opportunities, and unnecessary frustration—that is, if any real marketing happens at all. The smaller your business, the more critical every step and the greater the need for confidence in each one. Confidence is born from clarity, so let's get clear.

If I asked you to define marketing, what would you say?

When I ask a room of seminar participants to describe their idea of marketing, the common answer is always advertising. Most realize that marketing isn't exactly synonymous with advertising, but it's the only concrete way they know to describe this nebulous term that gets thrown around in a wide variety of contexts.

Ask anyone who sells radio or billboard advertising what they do and they'll likely say that they are a "marketing consultant." Ask someone who develops brochures and Websites. Ask someone who sells personalized mugs and t-shirts. All will likely tell you "marketing consultant" or something not too dissimilar.

From my lens, it seems the world is somewhat baffled by the concept of marketing whether it knows it or not. Collectively, we may never have had it straight anyway, and with the speed at which the marketing landscape is changing, it is becoming harder to know what to do and where to allot our resources. We have just cause for confusion. However, we must hold firm and steady on our quest to be smart and aggressive marketers. Survival is always at stake, and marketing is our greatest armor. With the proliferation of small businesses and independent entrepreneurs, all trying to survive in a hypercompetitive marketplace, we are called more than ever to get our marketing act together.

No doubt that can be challenging. There is a lot of skewed thinking and misinformation lurking in the collective consciousness of the business world. So let's hit the reset button. If you are to be a marketing machine, if you are to stand out, and if you are to make your marketing automatic, then you're going to need a fresh perspective and a new slate. Let's address some of these misconceptions head on by getting clear on what marketing is, what it isn't, and what it really means for your business.

Getting Straight on Marketing

Do you need to get your thinking straight? See how you fare with these common and costly misconceptions about marketing.

"Marketing" is not synonymous with "advertising" or "sales." These terms are mistakenly interchanged by marketers and non-marketers alike, but each is a separate and distinct function and must be treated as such.

They are akin to each other and should be used collaboratively as I will explain in detail shortly. For now, consider advertising and sales to be the offspring of marketing.

Marketing is not just what you do "out there." This is an eye-opener for many people. How about you? When you think of marketing, do you think about everything you do day-to-day *inside* your business as a means of marketing your business? Negligence of what you do internally undermines all of the hard work you do externally. This is uncharted territory for many companies, but it's like striking oil when you figure it out. Companies who operate strictly from an external marketing standpoint are operating half-mast. They are leaving tons of marketing opportunities on the table and working much harder than they need to. If this is you, you're about to hit the jackpot because I am going to outline for you in great detail how to capitalize on the marketing goldmine in which you're working every day.

For now, take a look around your business. Think about what happens every day as you service customers and perform standard operations. What are the events, tools, and common exchanges that impact what customers think of you? That make you attractive to prospects? That open doors for more opportunity? These are clues to what can become great marketing moments for you.

We will dive deep into this subject in the coming chapters. For now, let it sink in that marketing encompasses everything you do both outside *and inside* your company. This means you have far more marketing tools to work with than you likely realize—many that cost you little or no money. I'll teach you how to find them in Phase 4.

> *Negligence of what you do internally undermines all of the hard work you do externally.*

Your targets *want* you to market to them. Yes, you read that right. If you offer a product or service that improves the lives and businesses of your target audience, then they want to know about it. Targets may not be ready to act right away, but when they are ready, they'll want to know where to go. Customers generally like to buy from someone they know. (Don't you?) There is comfort in familiarity, even if their only experience is pulling your flyer from the doorknob and glancing at it on the way to the trashcan. At least they know something about you when they know nothing about everyone else.

If you are hesitating to tell your story because you are concerned about "bothering" people, then you need to shed that thinking right now—unless you don't want to be concerned with having any money. One step removed from bothering a target is ignoring a target. Most critically, if targets aren't getting your story from you, then you can bet they're getting it from your competition. Why leave anything to chance? Take charge of your message. Your targets want to know if you can help them, so tell them.

You cannot be everywhere so stop trying. Sometimes we marketers just need to calm down. We get all worked up about the latest marketing tools and technological advancements that can help us spread our message broader and faster with ultimate coolness. Accept that you cannot be everywhere and do everything, even if you did have the money. The world is moving too fast. Too many minds are at play. There is no keeping up, only more chasing and diluting your hopes and resources. Do what makes most sense for you and forget about the rest, even if it does make you uncool. Do fewer things well and do them better than everyone else.

More than ever, we are called to edit where we put our time and attention, to focus on that which gives us the best returns with the most speed and surety. A well-crafted, well-tracked marketing program like the one I will teach you in Phase 4 will help you immensely, though you'll still need a heavy dose of restraint. Just remember that one thing working perfectly is better than 10 working halfway.

Marketing comes with a guarantee after all. It is commonly said that marketing comes with no guarantees. What in business really does? There is, however, a guarantee that if you don't market yourself well, you will lose. You may not lose your business, but you will lose potential. You will lose costly hours and precious effort to replace business and generate more from scratch. You will lose momentum to help you push forward faster. When it comes to guaranteeing success, the answer could be grim if you rate marketing by each independent endeavor. But when you take a birds-eye view and consider its enduring, accumulated achievements, the results are seldom disappointing.

Marketing can be far more predictable than it gets credit for. It is seldom a mystery why successful companies achieve what they do, and why unsuccessful companies flounder. Those who complain about marketing generally are not doing marketing, or doing it well. Those who think, act, and communicate like a marketer have grand stories to tell, at least overall and in the long term. Marketing can be as predictable as you want to make it. Make yours predictably good.

Buzzwords come and go, but principles are forever faithful. There always seems to be a new marketing buzzword. As of this writing, it's "drip marketing." There we go making marketing complicated again. As Shakespeare would agree, marketing by any other name is still marketing. Yes, you need to understand "new concepts," but I assure you, if you think like a marketer, you will see through the labels. You'll come to understand that the "new marketing" is just everyone else catching up with what you already know to be the basic laws and tenets of marketing. The methods for applying those principles will change rapidly. Tools will come and go, but principles will serve you forever, no matter what buzzword is attached to them today. Certainly you need to be awake and attuned to what is available to you and where your targets are going. In the early 2000's, no one thought about blogs or online social networking groups as tools to generate business. As long as your marketing machine is driven by principle, you can call it whatever you like.

Chapter 3

Marketing by Principle

Removing the guesswork

Marketing can be a deceptive character at times, even two-faced as it seduces us with its promise of hope and then rears its ugly head of uncertainty, guesswork, and inconclusiveness. No doubt it asks a lot of us. It calls us to be persistent while it toys with us to see how long we can hold out. Sometimes marketing can feel more like a game than a business model. But then, that's usually when we're operating on whim rather than principle.

In truth, marketing is a soldier of fairness. You invest in it, and it will give you great returns. Operate by its time-tested, fundamental truths, and it will always deliver as long as you give it adequate time to do its job.

Most companies don't understand this. It takes only a quick glance and a few seconds of interaction to discern that most companies have no real grasp of these principles, and that puts you at a tremendous competitive advantage. Be among the rare few who understand and live up to these principles and you will surely stand out, both as a company and as a marketer.

So what principles do you need to market by? Every discipline of marketing has its rules, but there are a few sacred tenets that permeate all marketing whatever its form. Before we delve into those, however, I must make one upfront disclaimer: In all marketing, it is assumed that there is a viable synergy between buyer and supplier in the marketplace, that there is substantive need and want for the services and products you provide. If there is no match between what you offer and what the marketplace needs or is willing and capable to pay for, then no principle and no marketing can save your business.

That said, your business can be transformed by the following doctrines. Hold them close, for they are your trusted advisors, your allegiant shipmates, and your safe harbor when the winds and waters of your market environment become turbulent. As long as marketing involves people communicating with people for the purpose of exchanging goods, services, and ideas, these are and must be your guides. Use them to their fullest measure.

Principle 1:   Everything is marketing.

Principle 2:   Everyone is a marketer.

Principle 3:   Marketing is not sales.

Principle 4:   It's not all about you.

Principle 5:   It's not just what you do, but how you do it that counts.

Principle 6:   Consistency and constancy are key.

Principle 7:   Marketing must be constant in thought and constant in action.

Principle 1: Everything Is Marketing

There's a sweeping statement for you. Nothing ambiguous about that!

This is the principle that rules them all. If you operate from the mindset that everything is marketing, everything in your marketing will fall into place. This is the fuel on which all marketing machines run.

To explain it, we will need to take a closer look at what marketing really is. The more places you look, the more definitions you'll find. Most will say something to this effect:

Marketing is: "All activities involved in the sale of products and services."

Although I do not essentially disagree with this explanation, I find it not particularly helpful and not at all complete. It's not exactly a guiding force when you're in the trenches managing a database, slapping on postage stamps, and trying to write the headline for your next e-mail blast. Plus, it wholly misses the point that everything is marketing. There is no separation of activities that are involved in the sale of products and services and activities that are not. All activities are ultimately involved in marketing. All activities are marketing activities—period.

For clarity, let's look at a more functional definition. I developed this early in my career to help my customers grasp marketing and practically apply it in the everyday nuances of running a business. It's a 45,000-foot view of how you operate and market your business with real-life considerations of your day-to-day. When you operate from this mindset, choices and decisions come easily. You are guided and directed in all actions large and small to build and perpetuate your business. Simply put, you can spend much less time banging your head against the wall. As I see it,

Marketing is:

> The process whereby we make impressions and create perceptions, so that the customer decides that we are his/her best choice for the products and services we provide.

What does this really mean for your business? Let's break it down.

Marketing is a process...

Marketing is ongoing and never-ending. It is a series of steps that most often take more time than we would like. Still, marketing demands and deserves its due. It usually takes a lot of work and a lot of time to turn oblivious bystanders into active participants, happy buyers, and raving fans—and keep them as such. You'll learn more about the exact steps in Phase 2. For now, accept that, like housework, your marketing job is never done. You are on a perpetual cycle of making and keeping people excited about what you do and what you can do for them. The good news is that you always have another chance to get it right or do it better.

Whereby we make impressions and create perceptions...

This is why everything is marketing. Every day in everything you do, and with everything that represents you, you are making impressions and creating perceptions. Every communication, interaction, exchange, piece of paper, electronic transmission—every single thing—sends a message that can help or hurt you. Everything you do outside your business. Everything you do inside your business—how you look, how you operate, how you price, how you package, how you deliver, how you answer the phone, your advertisements, your Website, your brochure, your direct mail campaigns, the efficiency of your point of sale, the cleanliness of your bathrooms, the sign on your door, and the pictures on your wall. Everything. No exceptions. Yes, whatever you're thinking, that's marketing, too.

Marketing is all-encompassing. It is "all activities." Everything that is you and everything that represents you makes an impression and creates a perception that will determine if the customer will decide to choose you or choose you again. This is a monumental paradigm shift for most businesses. It's a new way of thinking and definitely a new way of acting, but it's a sure-fire ticket to success.

When you accept that marketing is not something separate from you, but is in fact part of the DNA of your business, you start perking up to the details.

You pay attention to what you do and how you do it, to what you say and how you say it. You behave more mindfully and strategically. You alter your actions and decision-making on all fronts. That may sound a bit scary, but I assure you, it is the secret that can bring great fortune to your business. For the small business, this is particularly significant. You can magnify your marketing reach and effectiveness by capitalizing on what is already inherent in your business and right under your nose, often with little or no money. This is an untapped treasure for most businesses, and an effective platform for standing out from the crowd and the competition.

I must disclose, however, that this principle does come with a couple of drawbacks. First, you cannot get away with sloppiness anymore; shortcuts will cost you. They always have, but now you'll know it. Secondly, this new enlightenment can cause anxiety when you aren't able to quickly capitalize on all of these newly identified opportunities. This is definitely a sore spot for the marketing-minded, but let me encourage you to celebrate that which you have done and focus on that which you can do right now. Just keep working at it. And know this: There are by far more average companies than exceptional companies. You do not have to be perfect to make a great impression and to stand out. Do the best you can with what you have. It will be more than you have done before, and likely more than your competition. New thinking and new action at any level means new results.

So that the customer decides that we are his/her best choice for the products and services we provide.

Why are these impressions so important? Because the primary purpose of marketing is to achieve emphatic selection by the target. This is a key distinction between traditional sales and marketing where sales is focused on the endless pursuit of the purchase. Marketers operate on a different playing field. We want commitment. Sales is typically satisfied as long as money is exchanged. To the marketer, the sale alone is not enough. We do love the sale, mind you, but we accept that our job is never finished. First, we need the buyer to buy again. Then we want her to decide that she would never buy from anyone else. Then we want her to tell all of her friends how great we are and why they need to be our customers, too. In sales, any agreement will do. In marketing, we don't just want our target to squeak out a little yes. We want a jumping-up-and-down, ear-piercing, "Yes!" That's when the marketer has reached true victory.

The difference is notably significant. How many times have you said yes to a telemarketer or salesperson just to make them go away? Come on, you can admit it. I admire you if your will is greater than mine. I'm sorry to say that I've been guilty more than once. The telemarketers (or tellesellers as they should really be called) were doing a happy dance as they chalked up another sale. I, on the other hand, was scolding myself for being sucked into the forbidden sales web that I know so well.

The salesperson considers this a triumph. The marketer considers it only temporary gratification. The teleseller won the sale, but not the customer. There is an acute distinction between buyer and customer, and marketers want the customer. We understand that true customers can make our companies wildly successful and that they can compound our hard work and marketing impact by being another strong voice on the street. Marketers are on a chronic pursuit to motivate the ideal target to choose us and choose us again. And again. And again.

You Are Never Not Marketing

I get a chuckle every time I ask a business owner what his company is doing right now to market itself, and he answers, "Nothing." You are never not marketing unless you are out of business. You may not be advertising anywhere. You may not be sending e-mail campaigns or direct mail postcards, or posting videos online, but you are always marketing because you are always making impressions in everything you do every day. Everything is working for you or against you. Everything is being counted by targets either consciously or unconsciously—what you do and how you do it, what you say and how you say it, in everything that is you and everything that represents you.

You get to choose. You can operate with your marketing blinders on, leaving impressions to chance and happenstance, or, you can take conscious, deliberate action to make every opportunity, every message, and every detail serve you.

How to Make Great Impressions

Of course your goal is always to make great impressions and avoid anything that makes a bad impression, but what about those that are neither good nor bad? An impression that isn't bad isn't automatically good. If it falls somewhere in the middle, it becomes categorized as "indifferent," which is a big bundle of nothing special. Indifferent neither excites nor agitates. It just sits there.

Interactions, communications, and tools that do their jobs but nothing else are indifferent. They have no real marketing value, nothing to make a business memorable or special, nothing to drive emotions one way or another.

Indifferent is what you get when service staff carry about their duties while not being rude, but not being especially helpful either. It is the fax cover sheet that's pulled from the word processing template everybody uses. It's the standard greeting customers hear when they step into a restaurant and are immediately asked, "Table for four?" Personally, I am beginning to think my name is Table for Four.

Indifferent is the office adorned with the expected silk plants, abstract art, and popular magazines. Sure it appears professional, and before becoming an enlightened marketer, you may have thought that was enough. There is absolutely nothing special about an office that looks like every other professional office. It has zero marketing value with nothing to make it stand out, nothing to teach, and nothing to make a lasting impact on the visitor. We could switch the nameplate on the door and no one would be the worse for it.

Customers are swimming in indifference. Repeated research shows indifference is the overwhelming reason why customers leave companies every day. It runs rampant like bad mold. That can be a headache for us as customers, but as marketers, it's a great advantage. Stale, indifferent actions come from a mindset of indifference. The more indifferent everyone else is, the easier it is for us to stand out with our great impressions.

No matter how you look at it, indifferent is a marketing opportunity lost, and it's acceptable only if you want to be an average company. So how do you guard yourself from this boring, business-choking state of indifference? In everything you do and in everything you produce, you simply ask this all-powerful question:

How can we make a great impression here?

All of the previous examples could have been easily kicked up from indifferent to great if only someone cared enough to think like a marketer and ask that question. Walk around your facility. Click through your Website. Pretend you are a customer going through your purchasing process. Ask the questions, *How can we making a great impression here? And here? And here? And here?*

Every day in everything you do, ask this question. If you are choosing uniforms, ask the question. If you are picking paint colors, ask the question. If you are deciding which software package to buy, ask which will help you make the best impressions with your targets. Ask, ask, ask.

I Saw the Sign

It's much easier to find examples in the world of bad and indifferent impressions than those that are really great, but every once in a while a company really goes out of its way to make a customer smile. When that happens, you know there's something special about that company.

I received a telephone call from a new prospect asking me to work with the marketing department of her software development company. My schedule was already overbooked. I didn't have the time to dedicate to another large assignment, but the lady was so kind and obviously in a pinch. So I agreed to visit. I had coached myself though. I was ready to stand firm if I was concerned in the least with the commitment and demands of the project. So, with shoulders back and head lifted high, I boarded the elevator. I had my mental soundtrack playing and I was ready. But then I stepped off the elevator and there it was, the sign that read in bold letters, *Welcome Lauron Sonnier, Sonnier Marketing.* Immediately I was smitten. I knew there was something different about this company. Sure enough. There were many special things about this company. They had room for a little improvement, and I agreed to help them. All because of a little sign and one big impression.

The best part—all customers and visitors get the same treatment. No wonder this company consistently enjoys large profits.

What Kind of Impressions Are You Making?

Another productive technique is to give yourself a scorecard by rating on paper the impressions you are currently making in all areas of your business. Use the sample sheet on page 31 to guide you. Give each item a rating of Great, Bad, or Indifferent. I call this your GBI Index, and it's a simple way to give you a quick visual on how much attention you have or have not been paying to your many day-to-day marketing opportunities—and if you're operating as an average, poor, or extraordinary company. Take a good look at each item you scored indifferent and ask how you can make it great. For each item you rated bad, ask how you can make it great immediately!

One final note: Although I am sure you know this, let me reiterate that perception is truth to the beholder, whether it is accurate or not. If people perceive you as disorganized and incompetent, then for all practical and marketing purposes, you are disorganized and incompetent. You can fill in the blank with any other adjective, and it will hold true.

When you understand that everything presents an opportunity to increase the strength of your marketing impact, you gain an empowering sense of control. Marketing is no longer a mystical force that sometimes shines its light on you and sometimes doesn't. Marketing is "all activities," and most of them are small. We tend to pay attention to the big things like location and product mix, but the marketing gold usually lies in the details whose cumulative impact can be detrimental if ignored, but quite powerful if worked wisely.

In fact, marketing can be likened to the "butterfly effect," a concept based in Chaos Theory and derived from the work of scientist Edward Lorenz. As reported by Wikipedia: "The phrase 'butterfly effect' refers to the idea that a butterfly's wings might create tiny changes in the atmosphere that may ultimately alter the path of a tornado or delay, accelerate, or even prevent the occurrence of a tornado in a certain location. The flapping wing represents a small change in the initial condition of the system which causes a chain of events leading to large-scale alterations of events."

A meteorologist remarking on Lorenz's work said, "If the theory was correct, one flap of a seagull's wings could change the course of weather forever."

Like the flap of the butterfly's wings, small marketing impressions can make hurricane-strength impacts on your business. Take charge of the impressions you make in everything you do, every day. Get everyone in your company involved in asking and answering, *How can we make a great impression here?* Use the GBI Index tool to help you go from acceptable to extraordinary.

Summing Up

Marketing is inherent in everything we do both outside and inside our business. It is ongoing and never-ending. It requires us to make conscious choices and great impressions in everything we do so that the customer chooses us willingly and happily. When you think about it, it doesn't seem that complicated after all.

Rate Your Business

In each of these common areas of business, rate your marketing performance as Great, Bad, or Indifferent. Fix bad impressions immediately. Then get to work on turning indifferent impressions into great impressions.

Impression	Great	Bad	Indifferent
Company exterior	❑	❑	❑
Reception	❑	❑	❑
Customer areas	❑	❑	❑
Non-customer areas	❑	❑	❑
Restrooms	❑	❑	❑
Invoices, statements	❑	❑	❑
Estimates, proposals	❑	❑	❑
Product packaging	❑	❑	❑
Service support items	❑	❑	❑
Website	❑	❑	❑
Brochures and sales tools	❑	❑	❑
Business cards and letterhead	❑	❑	❑
Staff dress and appearance	❑	❑	❑
Professional demeanor of staff	❑	❑	❑
Customer service	❑	❑	❑

Note that this is only a small sampling of all the areas your business can make a great impression. More comprehensive lists of impression opportunities will be offered in Phase 4.

Principle 2: Everyone Is a Marketer

Just as everything in your business is marketing, every person is a marketer. People often pay lip service to this notion but, as a marketer, you must take it very seriously.

Everyone is a marketer in and for your business, no matter their position. There are no exceptions, and now you understand why—because everyone is making impressions and creating perceptions in everything they do every day. It makes no difference whether the employee ever interacts with a customer. If they are part of the company, they are part of your marketing—your shipping clerk, accounting manager, IT guy, shelf stocker, and resident window washer. Everything they do and how they do it makes an impression that can help or hurt you: how they look, the quality of their work, the words they use and the tone of their voice, the decisions they make on the fly, their response time and attention to detail. Every single thing and every single person impacts your target's decision to choose you (or choose you again).

This reinforces the fact that marketing is as much an inside job as it is an external tool. You could spend crazy amounts of money to drive business through your door, but it won't do a bit of good if your internal engine is impaired. Because all activities are driven by employees, all employees are marketers. Everything is marketing and everyone is a marketer. There is no arguing it.

In the Mind of the Customer, Each Employee *Is* the Company

I have been the customer of a particular bank for many years. My relationship with the company had been pleasant, but nothing special. One day I walked in to make a simple transaction, but things just didn't go well for seemingly no good reason. I became extremely frustrated and, as soon as I walked out the door, I said in a not-so-shy voice, "I hate those people!" Have you ever had an experience like that?

This was a company I had been loyal to for many years, but because of one negative exchange in a handful of minutes, the relationship and years of working together quickly turned sour. In a moment, the entire company was reduced to "those people." Because of one person, I now hated them all. Perhaps it had been the bank teller's first day on the job, or maybe she had just gotten yelled at or received bad news. Who knows? But at that moment, I knew I didn't want to do business with that bank anymore. I was ready to pull the plug on our long history because of that brief encounter over nothing significant. How fragile our relationships are!

The problem was that the bank had not worked to establish a strong emotional bond with me. It was just a group of people in a building going through the motions of handling stark transactions from someone who was called a customer, but who was really a stranger. It was a big vat of indifference, so when the relationship was tested, it had no backbone to support it.

Sometimes in my workshops and seminars I give attendees a second nametag and ask them to write the name of their company on it. Then I tell them to turn to the person beside them and introduce themselves using their company name instead of their own. I've been amazed at how much laughter this exercise has generated. People feel silly and slightly awkward announcing themselves that way, but they definitely get the message that they are more than just representatives of the companies for which they work. It's a lesson we must all embrace if we are to be marketing machines—that, in the minds of customers and prospects, we are not just representatives of the company, we *are* the company.

Just consider how we talk as customers. All the time we use the pronoun "they" to refer to a company when we were dealing with a single person. "They" said I couldn't do that. "They" wanted to charge me extra. "They" gave me a hard time.

Customers see the collective whole of the company. Oddly, sadly, we on the inside lose sight of the whole and focus only on the parts, but to the customer, the parts are the whole. Everyone is the company. I am my company. You are your company. In fact, you may be the very reason customers do business with your company.

> *You may be the very reason customers do business with your company. You may be the very reason they don't.*

You may be the very reason they don't. Same goes for everyone in your team.

Getting Your Marketing Team in Shape

To build a strong marketing machine, you need team members who can be great marketers doing whatever they do. That requires care and caution when recruiting new members and in teaching your entire team how to think and act like a marketer. Commit to these critical steps to build and maintain your collective marketing muscle:

1. Lead by example.

2. Get your team members laser focused on the real impact they have on customers and the business overall.

3. Define the respective marketing roles of all team members and hold them accountable.

4. Constantly teach, train, groom, and advance your marketing team.

Let's take a closer look.

Lead by Example

That's a no-brainer. If you want your staff to think and behave in a certain way, it must be clear that you do as well. You must think as you ask them to think, do as you ask them to do.

Keep Your Impact in Focus

Before your team can embrace the impact of their respective actions, they must understand the impact they have on your company as a whole. That means understanding the real value you offer to your customer and the real reason customers buy from you. It is easy for all of us, even owners, to become consumed with the endless details of the day and lose sight of the higher purpose of our business. When we keep our purpose in laser focus, life and business become better for our customers and ourselves. And, we become better marketers. So what is the real value your business provides for your customer? What are the real reasons customers buy from you over someone else?

I remember a time in my company's adolescence when the stress of a growing business started to wear on me. I spent my days overseeing the production of brochures, Websites, and marketing plans while also managing employees, serving customers, doing accounting, and generally trying to keep everything afloat. I was overwrought with details, people, calls, demands, and deadlines. One day I was bemoaning to a friend how my life had been reduced to discussions about typestyles, paper textures, and color charts. What was I doing? What was all that work really for? How had I arrived at such a valueless place in my career?

Thankfully, my friend wasn't interested in wallowing with me. Without thought or hesitation she said, "What are you talking about? You are helping tons of people realize their dreams. You are helping their businesses grow. That means they can employ more people who can then feed their families. Sounds like pretty important stuff to me."

Wow! What a smack on the head. Her words were a much-needed attitude adjustment. In an instant, I had renewed respect for the work I did and the customers I served—for the customers I had asked for and the work I had chosen to do. After that, the text I wrote flowed easily, my ideas got bigger, and I enjoyed every discussion about typestyles, paper textures, and color choices. I won't tell you that I didn't slip back into Complaintsville every now and then, but when I did, I brought myself back to that conversation to re-focus my purpose and reinvigorate my dedication to the real impact I made in the lives of my customers, their employees, my employees, and everyone involved.

In business and in life, we too often minimize or forget the impact we really have. Our reach is deeper and wider than most of us realize. Unfortunately it can take losing a loved one to understand this. Let this be a reminder to you that your business, and you, personally, have a far greater effect on the world and the people in it than you could ever imagine. Make it a good one and make sure everyone in your business understands the role they play in it.

Every Role Counts

Companies who instill clarity of purpose in their staff always have interesting stories to tell, such as this one about NASA. As the story goes, dignitaries were visiting the space center, and one asked a female custodian what she was doing. Her reply was, "I'm helping to put a man on the moon." Now that is true alignment with a higher purpose.

No job is insignificant or exempt from making an important and impressive impact on the value and experience a company delivers to its targets. Every person and every position counts. Everyone is a marketer.

Get Specific

To help your team members understand their individual effect on your company and your customers—and of course your marketing—you must get specific. Just saying, "You play an important role," won't tell them what they need to do or do differently every day. You must tell everyone how their respective role makes a difference. Better yet, have a dialogue with them where together you ask and answer these all-important questions:

▶ Why is your role important to the company?

▶ What happens for the customer when you perform well?

▶ What does it mean to "perform well" in your position?

▶ What happens for the customer when you perform poorly?

▶ What does it mean to "perform poorly" in your position?

▶ What do your duties really mean to the customer?

Drill down to the finest details. Every decision, action, and activity presents a marketing opportunity, and you must operate in confidence that each person in your company is taking advantage and making great impressions in everything they do. They must understand the real contributions and consequences of their actions. They must understand that what they do every day has meaning far greater and far more reaching than the tools they use, the items they handle, and the paper they push.

If a business owner and marketing professional like me can forget the big picture, certainly a lower staff member can. It is up to you to protect the integrity of your marketing machine by keeping everyone mindful and focused.

Narrowing the Gap

One of the easiest ways to instill and maintain awareness of impact is to narrow the gap between your staff and customers. Each group should feel like they are working with real people and not just job tickets, order slips, and someone "over there." You can achieve this in many ways, including:

▶ Introducing your staff to your customers even if it's just with photos and bios on your Website.

▶ Including lots of staff photos in external marketing tools to "put a face on your company."

▶ Bringing staff members of all levels to visit customers on-site.

▶ Actively inviting customers to your location and hosting annual meet-and-greet events such as open houses and holiday parties.

▶ Regularly sharing stories about customers with your staff.

▶ Viewing customer Websites as a group so everyone can see for whom they are working.

▶ Having staff members sit with customer service representatives so they understand the types of conversations that happen daily with customers.

▶ Sharing customer compliments with staff.

One company I know used a clever approach to drive home the point that it is indeed the customer who pays the bills. They invited a prominent customer on payday to personally issue paychecks. One by one, the customer called each employee's name, handed over the check, and said, "Thank you for all you do for my business." The pride of those employees was palatable, and the company made its point loud and clear.

You can tell employees all day long that the customer makes their job possible, but seeing is believing. You can tell them that their role is important, but until they witness it, touch it, and feel it some way for themselves, they won't fully comprehend it. You must make the point real by being specific, sharing stories, and bridging the gap between your staff and customers. One way or another, get your customer into every level of your company.

So What Is Your Impact?

What is the real impact you have on the lives of your customers? What is the value you give when things go right? When things go wrong? What does each staff member need to know in order to make great impressions on your customers every day in everything they do? If you aren't crystal clear, ask your customers. Then spread the word to everyone else in your company. Every single employee must be focused on the impact they have on the company and the customer.

Define Marketing Roles

If everyone in your business is a marketer, then each person must understand his or her specific marketing role. Companies usually do not define marketing roles, but everyone should. As a marketing machine, you must. That means you have to get clear—and of course get it in writing. Marketing descriptions don't have to be long or complicated, just present to demonstrate your commitment to the marketing cause, to keep everyone mindful of their marketing role, and to help you hold everyone accountable. Once devised, these definitions should become part of the official job description for each position.

Each role or position falls within one of the four core functions of every business: operations, business development, human resources, and accounting. Let's explore the marketing roles of each function.

1. Operations/Production

This is the primary function of the business. It is what the business does and what the customer buys from the company. If there is no match in what you do and what the customer needs or wants, then there is no exchange. The challenge for operations and production is to perform and produce consistently at the established standards. Poor performance in this area can be extremely costly. The most persuasive marketing cannot overcome chronically missed deadlines, poor quality, and messy processes. Errors here will scar customer trust and essentially unravel all of your marketing.

Therefore, the marketing role of each employee in an operations or production capacity is simply to deliver goods and services in the manner in which they were promised to the customer. Your operations team can improve your marketing effectiveness by:

▶ Keeping everyone informed when problems arise.

▶ Constantly working to improve processes, output, and efficiency.

▶ Educating other departments about the demands and details of operations.

▶ Maintaining equipment, systems, and procedures to prevent problems and ensure consistent performance.

2. Business Development

Business development is comprised of your sales team and dedicated marketing staff. There remains a lot of confusion regarding the roles of sales and marketing, but you will need to get the story straight to get your marketing machine humming. I will reiterate that sales is a tool underneath your marketing umbrella.

In terms of people, you must have a marketing driver and, ideally, a marketing team if your business is large enough to support one. You may then have a salesperson or sales team. All of these players must work collaboratively and in tandem toward their shared goal of generating business for the company. How fortunate is the salesperson who has a marketing team to keep prospects and customers warm. How lucky the marketing department who has a live, active salesperson or team to close the deals it warms up.

All business development players have a role to target ideal candidates, make great impressions, tell the company's story, coordinate efforts with one another, and overall build and maintain growth momentum for the company.

Your marketing staff may also take on additional titles such as "impressions police," educator, encourager, cheerleader, driver, planner, strategist, developer, and miracle worker.

3. Human Resources

Attracting the right employees for your company can be even more crucial than attracting the right customers. Every hiring decision is a critical move for the company and should be handled carefully and cautiously. Every new person alters the dynamics and performance of your business and marketing every day. Every person impacts the experience your company delivers to external and internal customers alike. A "warm body" is in no way acceptable. You must allow in only people who are aligned with the values, standards, and purpose of your company. So then, the marketing role of your Human Resources team is to hire and help retain the right people for your company. What is "right" changes once you start thinking and operating like a marketer.

To me, the tell-all is this: You should be perfectly confident to slap a big sign touting your company name and logo on every single person you hire. You should be completely at ease to send every team member to your biggest and best customers. Would you be confident to do that with everyone on your team right now? Would you proudly allow them to walk around introducing themselves by the name of your company, or would you wince and cover your head in embarrassment?

Anyone who makes anything less than a great impression for the company in what they do and how they do it is no longer qualified, no matter the position. Newcomers must be made aware of their marketing role from the very start. (Current employees should be told right away.) This will be easy once you update your job descriptions to include marketing roles.

A kind lady at one of my seminars shared an interesting perspective with me on employees. She said that she has come to realize that people are like math. Some are adders and some subtractors. Some are multipliers and some dividers. With every hire, HR professionals have an opportunity to add, subtract, multiply, or divide the marketing impact and effectiveness of the company. It is up to us to shield ourselves from anyone other than an adder or multiplier.

Attracting Ideal Staff Members

Your marketing strategy should include an action plan to attract and retain ideal staff members. This is an important component of your marketing and business success. Why would new candidates want to work for you? Why should current staff continue to work for you? You must be ready and able to tell them.

Your HR team can improve your marketing effectiveness by:

▶ Implementing smart marketing processes to attract and retain ideal job candidates.

▶ Revising employee job descriptions to include marketing roles and duties.

▶ Helping to create a positive and motivating work environment.

▶ Keeping staff aware and focused on company values and standards.

▶ Initiating marketing training programs.

▶ Helping to bridge the gap between staff and customers.

Of course employee retention and general happiness are an important aspect of your HR department's marketing role. You cannot make happy customers with unhappy employees.

4. Accounting

Most accounting managers consider themselves protected and void of all marketing responsibilities. Now you know that is incorrect. Anyone who handles money is certainly a front-line marketing player. It's time to take off the blinders. No more hiding in the corner. No more excusing your accounting team from accepting and proclaiming their significant role in the marketing of your business. I don't have to tell you how sensitive money issues are, but I will remind you that your accounting team is making critical impressions all day long that can greatly help or severely hurt you. Issuing and rejecting credit, sending e-mails and making calls about overdue invoices, and using those awful words, "That's our policy." Few aspects of your business can rile emotions like accounting can. I have seen just as much business lost by the accounting department as any other department.

Your accounting team must be unmistakable in their understanding of the significance and sensitivity of their role. They must be trained how to communicate with customers. They must operate with constant mindfulness about their ability to build or destroy relationships in a heartbeat. In no way can you allow your accounting team to operate in the shadows. Instead, put their influence to good use. Capitalize on it to lift and strengthen your marketing impact where it is least expected. Your accounting team can rev up your marketing impact by:

▶ Adding "warm fuzzy" messages to your invoices, statements, receipts, and other administrative tools. Simple notes like, "It's a pleasure to work with you," and "We are grateful for your prompt payment" go a long way.

▶ Putting a face on the department. Have accounting staff personally call or visit customers to officially introduce themselves. Feature their photos and bios on your Website. Have them send a personal note to new customers. Establish your accounting department as real, courteous, helpful people instead of just a voice on the phone or handwriting on a late notice.

▶ Establishing fair and flexible policies that assist relationships instead of restrict them.

▶ Teaching the accounting staff how to be effective communicators, especially in sensitive issues where emotions could flare.

▶ Getting your accounting team involved in company activities so customers can see that they aren't snooty bad guys after all.

Train and Advance Your Marketing Team

No marketing machine can be built without ongoing education and training. As owner or manager, it is your role to guide your team's thinking, to help develop their skills, and to hold them to the highest of standards.

First, they will need to fully understand what your company does and how it works. I'm amazed and appalled at how little some people know about the company for which they work. These people look stupid in the moment, but it's not their fault. Sure, they should be more curious about the place they go to every day, but it is up to the company to teach employees about the company. Every waiter and waitress should be required and assisted in tasting every item on their restaurant's menu. How can they really answer customer questions until they do? Every employee at every company should know the president's name and generally everything the company does.

Staff must be trained to be great marketers. They must have a real working knowledge of what marketing is and what it means for them every day in their respective duties. This is a new idea for most companies. Employees are not usually lead to think this way. You must take proactive steps to regularly teach your staff if you want them to be effective marketers for you, as they should be and can be. Defining marketing roles is a great start, but employees must be continually reminded and guided about the details that matter in their jobs day-to-day. Each activity and each situation presents an opportunity to make a great impression and make the company stand out. You definitely want to arm your staff with skills to make the most of those moments.

Take the time to teach your staff what you learn in this text. Show them how everything they do makes an impression that is either great, bad, or indifferent. Get them constantly asking, *How can I make a great impression here?* Make marketing a constant topic of discussion.

Marketing skills are life skills. They make not only better employees, but better achievers, husbands, wives, parents, members, buyers, and leaders. No doubt, the better trained your team, the better your company—and the easier and more successful your marketing.

I love a story told by sales and performance guru Zig Ziglar about training. He tells about a business owner who was really struggling over spending the time, money, and energy required to conduct some training for his team. He asked, "Zig, what if I train them and they leave?" To that Zig said, "What if you don't train them and they stay?"

We are all better served by continually honing any skills, but especially marketing skills. No matter how hard you work to keep your external marketing sound, your company will never reach its full potential if you don't have every single person on your team pulling in the same direction. Get everybody educated and aligned and watch the magic happen.

Principle 3: Marketing Is Not Sales

It befuddles me why there is so much bucking of heads between the sales and marketing departments. Everyone wants the same thing; they just go about it differently. But then, people are territorial and they don't always embrace differences. If you want to be a marketing machine, you must convince sales and marketing to kiss and make up. Your company has too much to lose by not joining these mighty forces.

I have been resolute in my stand that marketing and sales are separate and distinct functions and that marketing is the umbrella under which sales is one of many tools to drive business. Marketing is horizontal; sales is vertical.

These disciplines have been wrongly entangled because the business world has focused primarily on the external manifestation of marketing. So, for this section and this section only, we will focus solely on the external aspects of marketing—the traditional role of producing and throwing stuff "out there" to warm up prospects and generate leads. However you look at it, you still need to make marketing and sales work collaboratively and in tandem, though you may be surprised by some of the reasons.

A Case for Both

As a marketing machine, you definitely want to operate with the full firepower of a coordinated sales and marketing effort. Marketing lays a strong foundation for successful selling, and sales reinforces the message and work put forth by marketing. You need both, but you need balance. A tilt too far in either direction can weaken your position and limit returns. Marketing without physical sales support has to work harder and longer. A heavy sales effort with no marketing support leaves you susceptible. The big danger is that, when you rely solely or mostly on active selling, you start selling your salespeople more than your company. Let me ask you:

▶ Do you worry that your salespeople will take good customers with them when they leave the company?

▶ Do you have to work hard to save customers when a salesperson moves on?

▶ Why would you put the fate and success of your company solely in the hands of strangers you pull off the street?

That's exactly what you're doing if you do not have an active, conscious marketing machine running alongside your physical sales team. Every day companies worry and suffer when salespeople leave because of all the business they could or do take with them. Is that you? If you haven't been actively marketing enough, then you have good cause for concern.

The reason salespeople are able to "take customers" is because they have developed personal relationships with those customers while the company has not. You could blame the salespeople, but it's really the company's fault for not paying attention (and not thinking like a marketer). The customers have become allegiant to the person and not the company. Their perception is that the offerings of the "new company" are just as good as the old one, and the old one is not suitable without that particular salesperson there to care for them. The customer follows the path of least resistance, solidifying the fact that customers work with people, not companies. It also makes a strong case for making your company something special. The more extraordinary your company, the harder to leave it.

For this and other reasons, it is imperative that you make your business "human" to your customers, and that you maintain a healthy balance of sales and marketing efforts. Customers must bond with your entire company, not just one or two people. It is dangerous to operate any other way.

The good news is that, if you put all of the principles you are learning here into action, you can sell your company, not just your sales team. You can build company-loyal relationships and safeguard your business from the coming and going of sales staff. Your sales team is just one of many assets of your company. Be sure your marketplace is aware of all of them by keeping a strong balance and force of sales and marketing.

Selling Your Entire Company

So, how do you sell your entire company instead of just your salespeople? Try these tips:

▶ Be sure customers are hearing from the company regularly, both separate from and in addition to their sales representative. Keep many marketing tools and vehicles in motion to remain "top of mind" with all customers and prospects.

▶ Help customers make friends throughout your organization. Get everyone involved in building the company's bond with customers. Beyond your own security, customers will appreciate the convenience of having several go-to people when they have questions or issues.

▶ Jump in immediately when a salesperson leaves or announces she's leaving to maintain your customer-company bond and retain customer confidence.

▶ Implement a process to follow up with customers at least semi-annually to check satisfaction with their salesperson. Personality differences between customers and salespeople (or customer service representatives) can cost you good business. Customers who are unhappy with their representatives usually don't speak up. They are more likely to just go away. Carefully match personalities and do a periodic check-in with customers to make sure they're pleased with the people they're working with.

Comparing Sales and Marketing

To help you become better equipped in orchestrating these two efforts, let's explore other important differences between traditional sales and external marketing. There is no right or wrong, only different, but you will need to be aware of those differences as you develop strategies to achieve your marketing goals.

Traditional Sales		Marketing
Convinces targets to buy	↔	Motivates targets to buy
Event-driven	↔	Process-driven
Sells the salesperson	↔	Sells the company
Limited exposure and capacity	↔	Unlimited exposure and capacity
Greater resistance from targets	↔	Less resistance from targets
Instant gratification	↔	Long-term results
Extremely costly per contact	↔	Less expensive per contact
Takes persistence	↔	Takes commitment

Sales convinces targets to buy.

Marketing motivates targets to buy.

A die-hard salesperson will either flinch at the word *convince*, or pride himself in the ability to win people over. I don't know which is better, but I do know that, as a buyer, I don't want anyone convincing me of anything. I want to arrive at my own conclusion and buy for my own reasons. As a marketer, I understand that when people make their own decisions, they become more committed, and that's exactly what I want. If you are selling toys at the circus, commitment might not be a factor, but it is for most businesses. Again, there is no right or wrong way, only what is appropriate for your business and target audience.

Sales is an event.

Marketing is a process.

Sales tends to be more of an event, an exchange in person or over the telephone whereby the salesperson tries to make a purchase happen. Certainly sales can require several tries and a lot of work. In fact, studies tell us that most sales, especially business-to-business sales, occur after the fifth contact. Still, with sales, there is a level of closure that is not available in marketing, which we know is an ongoing and never-ending process. Even after a transaction is made, marketing has work to do. Sales can choose to hand off a customer and move on to conquer the next deal, thereby perpetuating the "win and pass" process. Of course there is no single model, but for all practical purposes, marketing is process-oriented while sales is event-oriented.

Sales sells the salesperson.

Marketing sells the company.

I cannot underscore this distinction enough. No doubt your sales team is a critical part of your marketing strategy. No doubt your sales team is to be respected and honored for its significant work and contribution, but it must not work alone. Let the collective marketing power of your company shine through. Help your customers see that they are supported by your entire team.

Sales gives you limited exposure.

Marketing can give you unlimited exposure.

These are just logistics, but they matter. With sales being a human sport, you are limited in how many contacts can be made by any one person. With marketing, your power to reach any number almost instantly has never been greater or easier. Sometimes the personal touch will be far more effective. Sometimes you will never be able to get through except via mail or e-mail. You know the answer. You need both working for you.

Sales is met with more resistance.
Marketing is met with less resistance.

Let's face it. Salespeople are not the most popular people. As customers, we will do anything at times to avoid being "accosted" by a salesperson—walk down a wrong aisle, ignore a ringing phone, tell them we can't talk because we're about to go into surgery (at home). As the saying goes, people like to buy but hate to be sold. Marketing, however, is met with much less resistance. We've grown accustomed to it. We expect to be bombarded by it everywhere we go. Sometimes we pay attention, sometimes we don't. Sometimes we act, sometimes we don't. If we like what's being promoted, we're happy it showed up. If we don't, the marketing goes straight in the trash or gets clicked away. Obviously there are pros and cons with each response.

Sales can give instant gratification.
Marketing creates long-term results.

All right, I know sometimes it takes a lot of work for sales to achieve instant gratification. Still, it's a privilege not so prevalent in the marketing world. In sales, you get to revel in the big win, the ultimate moment when someone says yes or hands over the money. You get to add another point on your scorecard, and no one will quibble whether it counted or not. In marketing, we have to learn to get excited about much less. We take joy in every inquiry, response, and customer compliment, even if it doesn't go anywhere. The fruits of our labors aren't always obvious, and we have to work harder to gain and maintain momentum. Sales gets immediate feedback. Sales has more opportunity to enjoy the here and now while marketing must stay focused and hopeful on the future.

Sales is extremely costly per contact.
Marketing is far less expensive per contact.

Because humans are involved, personal sales activities are always going to be somewhat costly—as much as $99 to $450 per personal contact by some estimates, with numbers rising each year. Companies have to commit to the cost of salaries, benefits, and standard expenses that accompany any employee. With marketing, it is possible in some cases to achieve a per contact cost of just pennies. Plus, you can maintain full control of your expenditures, gauging, and gearing efforts around available resources.

Get Sales and Marketing Working Together

Your sales and marketing teams have every reason to be best buddies. There are no two departments who can support each other more than these. For the good of your sales team, your marketing team, your company, your employees, and your customers, get these two collaborating. Here are a few tips to help you do it:

1. Get both groups talking before you launch a marketing initiative. Your salespeople are intimately familiar with what the customer wants. Your marketing staff needs that information. Get these forces working together when it matters most—before the fact.

2. Keep salespeople informed of everything the customer could see. It is embarrassing how many times salespeople have been taken off guard by a customer who knew of a promotion before they did. Never let this happen! Anything going out to prospects, customers, or the marketplace in general should hit the desks of the sales team first.

3. Hold routine meetings to keep sales and marketing teams talking regularly.

4. Teach your sales team how to think, act, and communicate like a marketer. Everything you need to know to execute your marketing strategy, your salespeople need to know in the field.

5. Help the sales team develop common communications like thank you notes, meeting follow-up messages, and presentation materials. Why let all of your marketing talent go to waste with so many tools to be produced?

6. Support and respond to salespeople when they say they need something to do their job better.

7. Constantly feed salespeople great marketing ideas to make their job easier.

8. Cross-train each team. The more they know about the other function, the better they can support each other. Have marketing staff accompany salespeople on sales calls and have salespeople participate in marketing activities.

Sales takes persistence.

Marketing takes commitment.

With the ability for closure and the benefit of feedback, sales tends to have a more definitive set of steps to follow, and as long as it persists, it will either succeed or it will know there is no chance of succeeding with a particular target. Marketing operates in a more nebulous world where some things cannot be known, no matter how masterful or well-tracked they are. Therefore, the marketer is called to have great commitment, sometimes driving in the dark, but always knowing that with constant and consistent action, dividends will yield.

Principle 4: It's Not All About You

Your business may be yours, but it's not all about you. It's about your customers, the ones you rely on to feed your pipeline with their money. It's also about your employees, your vendors, the media, the public, and anybody else you need to help you achieve your goals.

Whomever you are trying to attract, motivate, impress, recruit, or otherwise win over is really the one calling the shots. There is nothing new or revolutionary about that, but if you look around, it's obvious that a lot of people still don't get it. They know it in concept but not in practice.

Take the average restaurant. There are always signs barking commands at well-paying customers. *No checks! No substitutions! Reservations only! Do not dare talk to us until your entire party has arrived!*

Why so angry? Didn't they want us to show up? Didn't they ask us to be there? We come with money!

How about the standard brochure? We could walk into any print shop in the world right now, grab a brochure from a variety of companies—plumbing, insurance, gasket manufacturing, dentistry, home building, whatever—and find that most just gloat about how great they are. So many years of experience. All that dedication and commitment. As a customer, I'm wondering how they think I have time for all that.

So let's get down to the facts. Your target audience is selfish. All target audiences are. They don't care about you, only what you can do for them. However you execute your marketing, it must be wholly directed at addressing the questions, needs, interests, concerns, and wants of your target audience. If you aren't operating your business from an "it's all about the customer" standpoint, you soon may not have that many customers to worry about.

Countless failed and floundering companies have learned this lesson the hard way. They spent too much time looking in the mirror rather than paying attention to the customer. Your eyes must be forever fixed on your customer. There is no more relevant picture. All things must flow from there. How do you do it? One way is to ask more smart questions such as:

▶ What is important to our customer here?

▶ What does our customer want?

▶ What does our customer not want?

▶ How will this benefit or impact our customer?

▶ What does this really mean for our customer?

You must know the answers to these questions in no general terms. In all cases, you must know specifically what matters to your target audience because that is what must matter to you, that is what must shine through in all of your marketing messages and in every detail of operating your business. If you don't know the answers, ask your customers. You may be surprised at what they tell you.

I experienced my own eye-opener when I heard an interesting story from a CEO of an advertising agency that helps large retailers attract ethnic buyers. The company takes a fresh and fascinating approach to really learn what matters to this target audience. Instead of the traditional surveying, they actually go to the homes of consenting subjects with a long list of questions and a video camera to understand their product usage and buying habits. And they uncover some very interesting things.

In one study, agency researchers learned that a particular ethnic group tends not to use dishwashing machines, even if they have one. The researchers would find dishwashers turned into storage bins for groceries, kitchen items, even clothes. For eating, the subjects used paper goods in large quantities. What researcher would have ever thought to ask targets if they used their dishwashers for any purpose other than dishwashing? By digging deeper, asking questions, and getting up close with their subjects, researchers were able to uncover amazing data that opened up tremendous marketing opportunities for a particular paper goods supplier.

In the end, everything you do must be done for the customer and with the customer in mind—absolutely everything. There is nothing in your business that is solely about you—not your administrative details, not the software you use, not your employee benefits and incentive programs. Every single tool, decision, policy, and protocol in your business becomes part of what you offer, the impressions you make, and the overall experience you deliver to your customer.

How many times have we as customers had to stand around the checkout counter or hang on the phone for a few extra minutes while staff negotiated their computer system? How often have we had to listen to employees complain about their work situation or the customer before us who ticked them off? How often do we read and hear the same marketing hash that tells us tons about the company but nothing directly meaningful for us?

I received a postcard from a real estate company and I wasn't sure whether to laugh or be sympathetic. The postcard featured an image of the company's very large, decaled vehicle with a dominating headline that simply read, *Trust Us*. The only other text was their phone number and address. Sorry. No chance of my ever trusting you. You're obviously too caught up with yourself. That's a terrific example of what we see in marketing all the time—people just talking about themselves while their target laughs and says, "Who cares?"

Everything is marketing and everything must be considered with your customer in mind—down to the very last administrative and operational detail. Your business is never all about you.

Principle 5: It's Not Just What You Do, but How You Do It That Counts

I have long preached this concept because I think people become too focused on the "what" and not enough on the "how." A lot of people serve food, but there are dramatically different ways to do it. Today it is all too easy for others to copy what we do. The better our business idea, the most assuredly it will be duplicated. But "how" we do what we do is not so easily copied. Therein lies great opportunity for us to set ourselves apart and stand out.

There are a lot of "how" opportunities in any business: How you engage a customer, how you deliver your product or service, how you handle complaints, how you make customers feel when they work with you, how you answer the phone, how you do everything.

If you're just going through the motions of delivering a standard product or service in a standard way, then you are, well, standard. You can't stand out by being standard. You need a good twist, a good "how" to pull you out and lift you up. Your ability to shine lies in not just what you do, but how you do it. Phase 3 reveals the four essential methods to standing out from the crowd, the clutter, and the competition. For now, you can simply ask, *How can we make a great impression here?* to unfold many great ideas to distinguish you from the pack. In truth, it doesn't take much to make a big difference.

Consider my favorite fast food restaurant, Chick-fil-A, for example. I really like the chicken there. I don't necessarily like the higher prices (hey, it costs more money to get real chicken), but I very much like the experience I get every time I go. Usually I'm hitting the drive-through, and usually the line is very long. I would be deterred anywhere else, but I have come to learn through consistent experience that Chick-fil-A knows how to move cars quickly. Not only that, they know how to turn every moment into a marketing opportunity. Once while I was making my way through the drive-through, a manager and another worker, both in neckties, walked the line passing out small cups of milkshake. Obviously that was a great and memorable experience, and it took little effort from them.

There are many great things to tell about Chick-fil-A. It's obvious they are thinking like a marketer and that their team is well trained. My experience with the company is consistent no matter which restaurant I visit. The company has standardized how they serve customers, but there's nothing standard about it.

When you order, you notice a special politeness about them. Their words are carefully crafted to make a common drive-through experience not so common. In the typical course of ordering fast food, we visitors are generally asked one of two things: "Anything else for you today?" or the extra warm, abbreviated version, "Anything else?" At Chick-fil-A, things are different. They ask, "What else *can I get* for you today?" It may seem like a subtle difference, but it means the world to me. Instead of an apathetic, "What else do you want?" approach, Chick-fil-A takes an active stance of service by asking what they can do for me. It's a refreshing change and it definitely gets my attention—just like after I thank them for my food and they say, "My pleasure." No, Chick-fil-A, the pleasure is all mine.

You would think if you could find this kind of attention at a fast food restaurant, you could find it at a day spa where the agenda is all about making the customer feel good. Not so with a particular spa in my neighborhood, an especially fancy one with rates to match. I have had the good fortune of visiting this spa a few times for a wonderful, relaxing massage. My last visit, however, was not so therapeutic. It was my fault, though. I arrived six minutes late. Yep, six minutes, and they turned me away. They asked me if I wanted to reschedule for the next day with no sense of regret or awareness of how utterly silly and rude they were being. No trying to make it work. Nothing. They had their secret rules and that was that. There was no offering to cut my services short. There was no consideration that every time previously, I was left in the waiting room for at least 15 minutes to catch up on the latest Hollywood news. What was good for the goose obviously was not good for the goose masseuse. I figured if they didn't have six minutes worth of flexibility, they didn't deserve my money. That was it for that salon. They won my business on their "what." They lost it because of their "how."

Market the Process as Well as the Product

Too often companies focus on selling the product when it is actually the process that distinguishes them from the rest—and that really matters to the customer. Take a real estate agent, for example. Ask any agent why you should hire her over someone else and she'll likely tell you that she'll sell your house fast at the highest price possible. Sure, that is what all home sellers want, but is that really why one agent would be better than another? Isn't that the job of a real estate agent anyway?

The missing component, and key marketing advantage, is the process. If you have ever sold a home, you know there are many factors that can make the experience like heaven or like hell, such as how well the agent understands the market. How aggressive a salesperson and marketer she is. How wide her network is. How sharp her negotiating skills. How astute her understanding of contracts. How large her budget to promote your listing. How well she keeps customers informed along the way. How well she can write up a sales sheet on the property. Many "how's" affect the end result and overall experience of working with one agent over another.

With this professional and many others, the job *is* the product. You sell the house. You prepare the tax return. You fill the cavity. You do what you are there to do. But your customers aren't just buying the end result, they are also buying the process. They might not realize it when they first choose you, but no doubt the experience of the process will be a major determinant of whether they choose you again.

This is an exciting opportunity for your business—to stand out by concentrating on that which matters to your targets and that which is overlooked by most companies. Set your mindset and day-to-day actions to concentrate on the process as much as the product, and then tell your story relentlessly in your external marketing. Focusing on the "how" just might be one of the easiest ways to differentiate yourself, and your customers will definitely love you for it.

Principle 6: Consistency and Constancy Are Key

Consistency is what breaks through and makes your message stick. Constancy is what keeps people thinking about you. These are your trump cards. Even the weakest of messages can work if you deliver it consistently and constantly. I have seen it happen many times. On the contrary, the greatest of messages will fail you if you don't get it out there often enough. It is repetition that gives the message strength.

Sporadic messages and false starts only waste resources. Marketing needs time to work. It takes time to build momentum and even more to maintain it. You cannot achieve this if you are constantly starting and stopping and throwing new or mixed messages at the marketplace. You must deliver a consistent message in a consistent manner and you must get it out there constantly—relentlessly. That is how I helped that mature company double sales in four years on a bare-bones budget and no outside sales staff, and that's what can catapult your business, too.

Why are consistency and constancy so critical? Because people forget fast. We live and work in a noisy, over-produced marketplace packed with marketing messages. There is little free space. As a marketer, I applaud entrepreneurial creativity and aggressiveness. When I see marketing on the side of a school bus, in the turnstiles at a sporting event, and on the back of a bathroom stall, I know someone is thinking like a marketer and recognizing opportunity where others see none. I know someone is wisely asking that all-powerful question, *What is the marketing opportunity here?* and I salute them. However, as a human walking amid the onslaught of hits, pings, and bullets, I'm tired. There is too much for me to pay attention to, so I miss a lot. If somebody wants my attention, they are going to have to keep asking for it.

There are other important reasons to remain consistent and constant. It keeps your story top-of-mind with targets. By showing up all the time, people are more likely to think of you first when they want or need what you offer. It gives you a competitive advantage and helps you weather the rough times. In business, you absolutely must be present to win, and it is often the last one standing who gets the prize. You have to show up and keep showing up. Even though people may not be ready to buy today, they may be tomorrow. Life is in constant change. Divorce attorneys never know when they may be needed, but having a permanent placement on television or on the back of the telephone directory puts them in front of targets when spouses are ready to call it quits. It's the consistency and constancy that make their marketing work.

Your objective is always to be there when targets need you, and the only way to do that is to be there all the time. If your message is consistent, targets will come to know and recognize you even at a quick glance or listen. Most of the time, that's all you get anyway, so you need to make it work. Consistency is the key.

Your message must be consistent in every respect—placement, message, tone, personality, presentation, color, typestyle, everything. If you were able to collect all that is you and all that represents you on a table—every brochure, advertisement, Web page, specialty item, administrative tool, everything—where you could view it all side-by-side in a high definition, widescreen perspective, everything should look like it was produced from the same hand, same cloth, and same company. Would yours?

Consistency of Experience

Chick-fil-A achieved consistency of experience by pre-thinking and standardizing every detail and every customer interaction. The experience customers have with the restaurant is consistent every time. Such must be the case with your business. How customers experience your company each time shapes their perception of you and the story they tell about you.

To make sure you're telling the right story and a consistent story, you must establish systems, protocols, language, and tools to standardize what you do and how you do it. You have to diligently train staff to make sure that the experience is the same every time, so it becomes part of who you are.

You'll learn more about this in upcoming sections. In the meantime, think about a great experience you had with a company. For me it was a visit to a new doctor. I had to wait all of two minutes to be seen. I was floored. The waiting room was warm and inviting. Every step of the process went quickly and smoothly, but not overly rushed. People were completely relaxed and gave me their sincere, undivided attention. It was the most delightful experience I have ever had at a doctor's office. I was excited to tell my friends about it. I was also a bit skeptical, because that's just not how things typically go when I visit a doctor. I paid extra close attention during my second and third visits. The experience was the same every time. As a customer, I am completely sold and freely tell my friends why they need to visit that office, too.

But what if I go back and things don't happen like they did before? I would be disappointed. The service by all measure and comparison could still be quite good and above average, but if it's anything lower than the standard the company has set for itself, then it will make a perceptively bad impression and shake my confidence in them.

Even great impressions can harm us if they are not consistent. In all things, be consistent and constant.

Principle 7: Marketing Must Be Constant in Thought and Constant in Action

You must always be thinking marketing so that you are always doing marketing. In Phase 6, we will review ways to help you maintain a marketing mindset throughout your company so marketing gets done and gets results.

▪

There you have them—the principles that should forever guide your marketing, and those that will get you thinking like a marketer and turn your company into a marketing machine. Are you ready to put them into action? Consider the questions you see here and at the end of each chapter to help you put your new learning into practice.

Something to Think About

▶ Which principles are you applying right now and which do you need to kick into action?

▶ What would be the most important principle for you to focus on right now to advance your business?

▶ How much of your marketing is focused on what you do inside your business?

▶ What is the real value and impact your company provides your customers and your marketplace?

▶ Is your company guilty, like most companies, of making lots of indifferent impressions? Any bad impressions?

▶ Where can you turn some indifferent impressions into great impressions?

▶ How can you get your entire team asking, "How can we make a great impression here?"

▶ Is every team member a strong representation of your company?

▶ How can you start training your team on these important marketing principles?

▶ Are you getting your marketing and sales functions confused?

▶ What do you need to do right now to get your marketing and sales teams working together productively?

▶ How consistent and constant are you? What improvements can you make?

Tips 1–10 to Help You Put Marketing Into Action

1. **Make working with you effortless.** Perfect the process of working with you so that it is abundantly pleasant and easy. That will always get people talking.

2. **Never, ever underestimate the power of a contact.** You can never know who could impact your business today or tomorrow. Treat every person you encounter with respect. Give them your attention and make a great impression on them. Teach them about your company and leave them with something to remember you by. You never know who they are married to, who they know, or when your paths may cross again. Never, ever underestimate the power of a contact.

3. **Cross-promote departments and offerings.** Does everyone in your company know everything the company does? They must. They must be aware and well versed in all that the business offers and how it works. They must know how to identify and respond to opportunities to cross-promote departments, products, and services. Hold info-sharing sessions, cross-train, and teach everyone how to sell the entire company, not just what they do.

4. **Make prospective employees love you.** The principle of never underestimating the power of a contact applies to prospective employees as well. Whether they are suitable for your company or not is immaterial. They will likely share their experience with others, maybe many. Your goal is always to make great impressions, no matter with whom you're dealing. Treat everyone with courtesy and respect and be extra tactful in delivering bad news.

5. **Invite only ideal people into your circle.** The quality of your company, your offerings, and your life depend on the people with whom you interact daily. Get rid of toxic customers, vendors, and employees. List on paper the "ideal profile" for each of these core target groups and anyone else important to your success. You're more likely to find and attract the right people when you know who they are.

6. **Make your receptionist a marketing machine.** This "first impression" person is critical to your success. Hire extra slowly and carefully when choosing the first voice, appearance, attitude, and mentality that prospects and customers encounter when they approach your company. Test candidates in real life situations before hiring. After hiring, train, train, train. This person can make or break business all day long.

7. **Keep your receptionist in the know.** As the most universal point of contact with prospects and customers, your receptionist needs to know what's happening in the company. Acquaint her with all people, areas, and functions of the business. Keep her informed of promotions, events, major Website changes, marketing activities, and any other details that callers or visitors might ask about. Your receptionist should be a good voice, a good marketer, and a central source of information for everyone.

8. **Impress them with what you do for *them,*** not what you do for you. Improvements in your business may be for you, but they should always be marketed in terms of what they do for your customer. Updating your computer system or moving into a high-profile office building may have given you some new tools and a beautiful place to work, but your message must be focused on its outside benefits such as quicker processing or easier access. Marketing must always be about the customer.

9. **Don't make them wait on you.** Nobody likes to wait, whether to receive a product or service, to be acknowledged at the counter, or to have their phone call or e-mail returned. Be acutely conscious of the

amount of time you're making prospects and customers wait in all aspects of doing business with you. Establish the values, systems, standards, and tools to keep waiting time to a minimum. Respect your customer's time in every way. Even taking a phone call during a meeting is making your customer wait on you (and it's rude). Where are you keeping customers waiting and how can you fix that?

10. **Develop common answers to common questions.** You know what customers commonly ask, so be ready with an answer. These moments present important opportunities to make great impressions. With your team, identify the questions and craft the best words and practices to address them. Take charge to ensure that your company responds in the best manner possible, consistently.

PHASE 2

Stir the Pot

Nothing happens until there's motion.

Chapter 4

Putting Marketing in Motion

The magic of stirring the pot

It is universal law that everything exists either in a state of circulation or congestion. Things are either in motion or stillness, in action or inaction, in fluctuation or stagnation. The air in your body, the money in your bank account, your openness to new ideas—everything is either flowing or it's not.

When things aren't moving, there's usually trouble. Lack of oxygen, money, and new ideas could no doubt be detrimental, even fatal.

Your business is no different. It's either flowing and advancing or it's still, stuck, and regressing. It's either making good things happen or it's brewing trouble.

> *Marketing is the mover. It's what keeps your business circulating. Stop actively marketing and you'll reach the perils of congestion fast.*

Marketing is the mover. It's what keeps your business circulating. Stop actively marketing and you'll reach the perils of congestion fast. No new business. No recurring business. No referring business. You'll become like the still waters of the bayou—festered by swarms of mosquitoes ready to take whatever life you have out of you. Take something as simple as cream in a jar. If it just sits there, it remains cream. Let it sit too long, it becomes spoiled cream. But give it a little shake for a few minutes, and you'll have rich, tasty butter ready for spreading on your breakfast toast.

The bottom line is that nothing happens until there is motion, and that magical, life-giving motion in marketing is what I call "stirring the pot." Of course I am a Cajun from Louisiana, and we Cajuns tend to put everything in terms of food. Still, in all my years of marketing, I have yet to find anything that so perfectly and practically captures the essence of marketing. When you actively market, you get circulation. When you don't, you get congestion. It's just that simple.

"Stirring the pot" is a powerful concept that can breathe tremendous life into your business. It makes marketing sensible and strategic. It gives you direction, removing the mystery of what you need to achieve in every step. It makes great things happen for you and your customers. So let's get stirring!

Discovering the Magic of Stirring the Pot

I originally learned about "stirring the pot" from my mother who could cook like a mad Cajun woman. She was always mixing up some fabulous Cajun cuisine like gumbo, sauce piquante, and étouffé. These dishes begin with a roux base, a mixture of flour and cooking oil that has to be stirred constantly until it is the perfect color and consistency. It takes about 45 minutes of constant stirring to get it just right.

I would often be recruited to help with the arduous task. Invariably, I would complain and want to stop, but my mother would just tell me to keep stirring. If I did stop, the roux would burn, and we would have to start over (and Mama would not be happy).

I must have been told to "stir the pot" about 5,000 times growing up with all the great cooking she did. I will forever hear the ring of my mother's voice telling me, "Stir my pot, Lauron. Stir my pot. Don't you let my roux burn. Keep stirring, Lauron. Keep stirring!"

Little did I know that my mother was teaching me a significant life lesson and a cardinal rule of marketing—that for anything to happen, there must be motion. It is the stirring of the oil and flour that make them blend into something new. With every lap around the pan, the work of the last stir becomes greater and more significant. Momentum kicks in, and each stir gets the cook closer to the consistency, color, and flavor that will make the perfect roux. With more stirring, the roux and water become gumbo as all ingredients get mixed together to create a delectable dish. Even after the gumbo is made, there's still more stirring to do. Take a little taste off the top of a gumbo pot without giving it a good stir first and see what you think of that! Suddenly Cajun gumbo won't be so exciting.

The Cost of Not Stirring

When a pot is allowed to sit with no stirring, either nothing happens or trouble happens. The parts remain separate and never meld. All of the good stuff sinks to the bottom while all the junk floats to the top—just like in your business.

Stop stirring your marketing and you will certainly see consequences. Less new business. Less repeat business. Fewer referrals. The wrong kind of customers. And a dwindling balance sheet.

When we think about it, a business is lot like a good gumbo. It requires diligent action to create a solid foundation. It contains lots of components that must be continually stirred. And, when it's done well, people smack their lips, talk it up, and beg for more. That's good gumbo-making, and that's successful marketing.

It Takes a Mix

By its very name, a gumbo is a mix of ingredients that, with some time, heat, and a lot of stirring, come together to create something new, wonderful, and life-sustaining. It requires some center stage items (chicken or seafood), some support items (onions and peppers), and some small but essential items (the must-have seasonings). Leave anything out and the gumbo isn't as tasty. Leave certain things out and it's not worth eating at all. But get everything in there working together and you've got what the Cajuns call *bon, bon, bon* (good, good, good).

The same holds true for your marketing. You will have major strategies, initiatives, and campaigns using a variety of marketing tools and methods. You will have supporting elements such as everything you do in your business every day. And, you will have a host of essential details that will enhance the overall richness and impact of your efforts. You need all ingredients working for you or your marketing gumbo just won't taste, or work, as well as it could. (By the way, if you haven't enjoyed authentic Louisiana gumbo, you owe it to yourself to seek some out. Just be sure it's the real deal.)

Whatever you're cooking in the kitchen or in your business, it's the motion that makes the whole thing happen. Time to stir things up!

Stirring All of Your Pots

No matter what kind of business you are, you likely have several pots on your stove. These "pots" are the many different target audiences you need to market to—new prospects, current customers, referral sources, vendors, associates, members, influencers, the media, and anyone else who can help you reach your business goals. You will also need a pot for your employees—your internal customers—and even one for yourself to help you keep marketing at the top of your mind and priority list. Each pot must be carefully and constantly tended. (Can't let that roux burn!) With so many pots, this may sound like a lot to juggle, but once you learn how to streamline your marketing activities in Phase 4, you'll find that stirring a lot of pots becomes not so difficult after all. For now, your task is to identify the pots you need on your marketing burners.

What pots do you need to stir?

Your Customer Pot

Fostering sound customer relationships must be a priority in your marketing strategy. It amazes me how much attention people place on getting new customers rather than keeping and nurturing the ones they already have. Business almost becomes an assembly line of pulling customers in, only to tick them off and ship them out. Bring them in. Tick them off. Ship them out. And around and around they go. What lost opportunities! What tons of money left on the table. What a waste of all that work to earn customers only to have to do more work and spend more money to replace them. It's like running in place.

Growing organically from what has already produced fruit is unquestionably the easiest way to expand any business. Opportunity just sits and waits to be taken. Why then is it so often untapped?

The answer is not logical, but it is understandable. It is, in fact, our own human nature that hurts us. It is the love of the hunt, the pursuit, and the thrill of the ultimate win. The problem comes when we get too wrapped up in the rush of the catch that we overlook what we've already caught. Yet again, people make marketing more complicated than it needs to be.

On countless occasions, I have complained to companies that they spend more time rewarding customers for becoming one than just being one. How can we speak about customer loyalty if we do not reward it when we get it?

Your marketing machine must be different. You must act on that which you know to be true: focusing on current customers is just as important as targeting new prospects, and usually a lot easier. You must execute an aggressive strategy to motivate and care for current customers so they will continue to choose you and choose you for more. Constant stirring is mandatory. Customers must be constantly told how grateful you are to have them, shown what else you can do for them, and nurtured to strengthen their ties to you. You need to keep making impressions and creating perceptions so customers remain firm in their decision that you're their best choice for all the products and services you provide.

Your internal customers, your employees, require the same attention. Now you understand how critical each and every team member is to your marketing success, and that means they are a target audience to stir and address in your marketing strategy. Of course you need to motivate and retain good employees. You want your staff interacting politely and productively with each other and with external customers. And, you want them to help you advance your marketing position.

By implementing a strong plan to keep both external and internal customers well stirred, you will be armed and ready to attract good talent and posture yourself as a true standout company.

Your Prospect Pot

Before you start stirring your prospect pot, you must be clear on who belongs in it. A true prospect is a buyer who wants or needs what you offer and has the capacity to pay. Even within your qualified target audience, there are some targets who may not be right for you for a variety of reasons, such as they are hard to please, they negotiate too hard on pricing, or they have projects that over-extend your capacity. Prospects can be like food. Some will nourish you; others will harden your arteries. By stirring your prospect pot, you can attract the right targets—those who are profitable and pleasant to work with—instead of just those who happen to float to the top or walk in the door. Create an Ideal Customer Profile that outlines all of the demographic criteria (such as size, sales, industry) and buying behaviors (such as ease of partnership, project demands, growth potential) that make a prospect or customer ideal for you. The better you identify your ideal targets, the easier it will be to find them.

For tailoring purposes, you may need to divide your prospect pot into smaller pots. Usually prospects, even the best ones, are not created equal and that means different marketing initiatives for different groups. As you develop your marketing strategy and your database, you will be well served to categorize your prospects so they can be easily extracted by some logical ranking. An A-B-C rating of the perceived quality and potential of prospects usually works well if that is possible. Or, maybe you need to divide your prospects by type or geography. Do whatever makes sense for your business, but know that some type of organization will be extremely helpful, if not necessary.

Tailoring programs to specific target groups is easy when you can single them out quickly.

Other Pots

There are other people who are significant to your success, and they should be dutifully considered as an important "pot" in your marketing strategy. This could include vendors, referral sources, and other influencers who can help direct or persuade business your way. It could be media, trade organizations, associations, and even the general public. Each business has its own combination of target audiences, but one target that must always be on the list is you. To keep your marketing strategy on track, you will need to keep marketing at the top of your mind. I'll give you specific tips on how to do that in Phase 6. For now, decide who else needs to be included in your marketing program to make it complete and comprehensive. What other pots do you need to stir?

Chapter 5

Stirring the Right Things

The five things you must always be stirring

Now that you have identified all of your pots, it's time to get stirring. But what ingredients, what elements, do you need in each pot? What exactly do you need to stir?

I have developed a five-step methodology to guide you through the complete marketing cycle, appropriately called the Stir the Pot™ Method. These five steps can turn an oblivious bystander (with potential of course) into a committed customer and that committed customer into a talkative fan. It is the ultimate success in marketing, the perfect gumbo.

Like all marketing, stirring the pot is a process, ongoing and never-ending. Once you lead a prospect and then a customer through all five steps, you simply repeat the process to keep your customer committed and spreading good cheer about you. Even then, you're not done. Any time you have something new to market, you need to take targets through the cycle with that message, even though you're still working on other steps. I know it sounds like it could be tedious, but I assure you it is not. There is logic in the order of these steps, but they are not necessarily sequential. Because everything in marketing is interconnected and interrelated, when you make achievements in one step of the cycle, you make progress in others. That takes the pressure off. As long as you keep the cycle in motion, and stir all five components, your gumbo and your business will be the talk of the town.

I have applied the Stir the Pot Method faithfully and have enjoyed terrific results for my customers and myself. It's an easy and effective way to get your mind and arms around what you must specifically accomplish in promoting your business. It's your foolproof recipe for marketing, no matter your type of business, industry, or marketing goal. Stir the Pot is the ultimate formula for making marketing work.

The Five-Step, Stir the Pot! Method

With every target, and with everything you do inside and outside your business, you must constantly and consistently:

1. Stir Awareness
2. Stir Emotions
3. Stir Mindfulness
4. Stir Conviction
5. Stir Word-of-Mouth

So get your big spoon ready. It's time to be a gumbo-making, business-building, killer marketing machine.

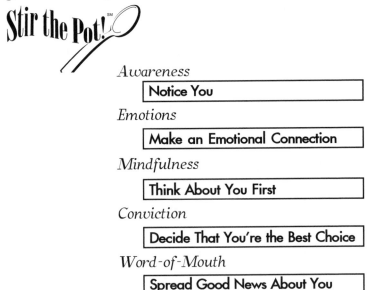

Stir the Pot!

Awareness
> **Notice You**

Emotions
> **Make an Emotional Connection**

Mindfulness
> **Think About You First**

Conviction
> **Decide That You're the Best Choice**

Word-of-Mouth
> **Spread Good News About You**

Stir Awareness

Everyone knows that marketing is all about building awareness, yet every day people sabotage their efforts to generate it. They get stuck in this stage because they don't apply the core principles of marketing that you've already learned, especially the principle that constancy and consistency are key. One or two little squeaks to the marketplace are just wasted effort. You need frequency and repetition to make your marketing work. So get your message out there and keep it there. Be the last one standing when your competitors have gone home. And stop changing things up so much. All of those stops and starts give your messages no time to stick or build momentum. Just because you have lived and breathed your marketing message for what feels like forever doesn't mean your targets have. Even if you told them a million times who you are and what you do, you must never assume they know. Again, targets forget fast. Their lives are full, and it takes a lot of work to break through the over-crowded, over-cluttered marketplace. Probably a lot more than you think.

Research tells us that it takes a minimum of seven to nine exposures of a consistent message within a reasonable period of time for the message to even hit our target's radar. Seven to nine times! Far too often, people give up much too soon. They abandon their marketing efforts after a couple tries, considering it finished when it is really just getting started. If you are operating this way, you are only inviting failure and wasting precious resources.

I have to admit that I too can be exhausted by the seven-to-nine rule. But I know that I will be stirring awareness forever. I devise my strategy, like the one you will learn in Phase 4, to ensure that all of my targets, my "pots," get automatically stirred on a regular basis.

Get your message out there relentlessly. Tell the same message both inside and outside your company. Don't judge an effort until you have had it out there long enough and often enough—at least seven to nine times in a reasonable period of time. What's a reasonable period of time? Every business is different, but generally consider how often targets buy what you sell. If you sell pizzas, then the pace of your marketing needs to be quick and steady, because people make food decisions every day. If you sell large machinery or a professional service that is purchased only periodically, you can disperse your direct hits at a slower clip such as monthly. Whatever schedule you determine is best for you, just keep it constant.

Building awareness is the first step to making anything real happen. You cannot achieve success in any of the other steps until you have someone's attention. However, the better you perform in the other Stir the Pot steps, the more easy it will be for you to succeed in this one. That's just the circular nature of marketing. As marketing unfolds, it compounds.

Stir Emotion

Stirring emotion is absolutely one of the most important and necessary steps in marketing, and often overlooked. Once again, other people's ignorance becomes your marketing opportunity.

People are emotional beings. We all make decisions based on emotions and then justify them with fact. Study after study has proved this. (*Sure, that hot sports car costs a lot more, but it will really hold its value when it's time to sell.*) Even the most analytical, left-brained engineer or accountant will choose a company or product for emotional reasons whether they know it or not. They may think and say their decision is based on fact, but in the end, the real trigger was the comfort or other feeling derived from that fact. How many times have you paid too much for something because you really, really liked it? How many times have you spent your money foolishly because of the delight it brought to someone you loved? How often have you agreed to do something only to make others think or feel better about you?

Evident or not, decisions are almost always based on emotion. All of us are in constant pursuit of pleasurable emotions and avoidance of painful emotions, and we make our choices and decisions accordingly. That is critical knowledge to remember as you work to influence the choices and decisions of your targets.

In the highly recommended book, *Why Customers Really Buy*, authors Linda Goodman and Michelle Helin explore real-life examples of emotions trumping reason in the corporate world. Armed with many years of research, they beautifully illustrate and support that:

"The motivations customers act on are seldom logical, predictable, or even conscious. Instead, their strongest responses stem from one source: emotion. It's a deceptively simple reality, one that the business world has resisted, preferring instead to concentrate on quantifiable explanations for customer behavior. But whether customers are consumers or other businesses, all customers are people. And people are emotional beings. Despite any posturing to the contrary, decisions are swayed by emotion. When this emotional dynamic is acknowledged, it changes the way organizations must go about understanding their customers. It changes the way companies must make decisions."

It also changes the way you must market.

Understanding What Emotions Matter

You cannot make a meaningful connection with targets until you are clear on the emotions that are important to them—the feelings that make them want or need your product or service. You must know how they want to feel when they do business with you, the kind of pleasure they are seeking or pain they are avoiding, what worries and excites them. If you don't know, then you must ask them. These emotions become your benchmark for all of your business actions and decisions and, of course, your marketing. Everything you do and how you do it becomes centered around making customers feel confident, comfortable, secure, joyful, relaxed, successful, free, frugal—whatever you uncover as their emotional triggers.

Making an Emotional Connection

Once you are clear on the emotions that matter to your targets, commit them to paper as a guiding Emotional Profile. You will need to visit all of your target groups to make sure you are clear on what matters to each. The desired emotions of your internal customers will likely differ from those of your external customers, but you can certainly expect overlap as they are all human.

Now you are ready to make big things happen. Empowered with the emotional triggers that can stimulate positive responses in your targets, you have complete direction for everything you do. And indeed everything you do must create the tone and atmosphere to stimulate those emotions. The words and images you use. The overall experience of working with you. Even the design style of your communications and the decoration of your office. Everything counts, only now the guesswork is dramatically reduced. Options are narrowed. Decision-making becomes far less overwhelming and considerably easier. You can operate with efficiency and an abundance of confidence. You get what all marketers long for—direction!

When you operate on marketing principles, ask the right questions, and work from a vantage point of sound knowledge, it's easy to know where to take your marketing. Working in the dark will never get you where you want to go. Stirring the right emotions will get you everything!

An Emotion We All Love

Of course love is the most powerful of all emotions, so show your targets you love them. Counselor Gary Chapman in his book, *The Five Love Languages*, outlines the five ways he contends we all demonstrate feelings of love—acts of service, words of affirmation, quality time, gifts, and physical touch. Although he focused on personal relationships, I think we would be wise to consider these languages as useful tools in our marketing. After all, we are just people relating with people. Working in the context of business calls for some revision, but no doubt expressing love in any way is sure to stir positive emotions. Doing so makes you a good-hearted company and a smart marketer.

Acts of Service—Customers always appreciate acts of service, but to get noticed, your good deed will need to go beyond what you normally do and what is normally expected. Create a culture of courtesy and kindness. Consider how you can develop a reputation for being supportive and helpful. Do you need to throw in a few freebies, not charge for something, go out of your way to help the customer even when it's not your duty? Use acts of service to show customers you are sincere in taking great care of them. Just be sure they know all you do for them.

Words of Affirmation—Couldn't we all benefit from more affirmation and encouragement? Your targets will love you for this one, especially your internal customers. Be prolific in serving up kind words. Give people an emotional boost with a compliment or vote of confidence. Congratulate all targets when they do a good job, no matter how minor. With customers, drop notes when you see their names in the media. Acknowledge their kindness in being organized to make your job easier. As the saying goes, *What you appreciate appreciates.* Want to be a magnetic company? Be a sincere source of information.

Quality Time—With customers, this is simply attention. Be reachable by phone. Make the effort to visit your target face-to-face. Drop e-mails regularly. Give targets your full attention when you're with them rather than check your watch constantly. Ask targets questions to demonstrate your genuine interest in them and then really listen.

I learned a valuable lesson about quality time from a VP at a major energy corporation. He was a customer and he always wanted to take extra time to chat about life, family, and movies. He was newly and happily married so there was no ulterior motive. Fortunately, I found him pleasant, but I tended to hurry our conversations because I assumed he was extremely busy. Frankly, I had just launched my business so I had no time to waste. After a few meetings with the same behavior, I realized that he just enjoyed talking. We would meet to do business for five minutes and then have casual conversation for the rest of the hour. I was frustrated at first. We could have done most of that work over the phone. But then I got it. He loved doing business with me because I would give him those 55 minutes. I would listen to him. No doubt he could have hired a hundred other companies to do the job we did, but he continued to choose mine because I gave him quality time.

In the rapid drumbeat of our lives, we forget the importance of taking a breath and lending people our ear. Sometimes the best marketing we can do is simply be quiet while our customers do all the talking. Just be sure to pick interesting customers.

Gifts—Everybody loves a present, and any shape, size, or price range will do. You can go deep with expensive sports tickets and rounds of golf, but don't think you have to. Sometimes you can accomplish just as much with a candy bar, party favor, or handwritten note. Gifts can be sent as promotions, thank you's, reminders, and "just because" you want to show a little kindness (and remind them of you). I maintain a gift box in my office where I keep a wide variety of supplies on hand for when I need to spread goodwill. If you were to dig in there right now, you would find inspirational cards and magnets, mugs, candies, stress balls, small hot sauce bottles, packaged rum cakes, beautifully framed four-leaf clovers, and a large slinky. Oh, and there is that fun replica of a high-heel shoe that I sometimes use to "get my foot in the door" with prospects.

You can purchase official advertising specialties emblazoned with your company name and logo. Just be sure they help you make the right point about your business. I love specialties, but sometimes they are hard to get on a limited budget or for small programs. In that case, I head to the party store where shopping is always fun and where I can pick up inexpensive items that are sure to get attention and help me make a marketing point—like those over-sized sunglasses that always get a laugh and help me tell people they need to expand their thinking about marketing. My favorite items are the little red plastic spoons I give generously to remind people to stir the pot. People have even asked for extras.

Gifts serve many good purposes. They make people feel special. They engage the senses with something to feel and touch. They hang around to keep targets thinking about us. And, in some cases, they make people feel almost obligated to give us something back. As humans, we have an innate tendency to reciprocate. Case in point: a performance survey conducted by one of my customers.

The company was administering written customer surveys through the mail and, to increase response, the company owner included a crisp one-dollar bill with each survey. The company received an impressive 70-percent response. The gift of the dollar made many respondents feel obligated to return their completed survey in exchange for keeping the dollar. One recipient humorously mailed back the dollar with a note saying, "I apologize, but I will never take the time to complete your survey. Here's your dollar back." Point made.

A sage person once told me that I should leave something good everywhere I go. I miss a lot of chances, but I score more than I lose. I leave physical gifts or just a compliment, joke, tip, good idea, word of encouragement, or word of thanks. Give gifts of any kind. Give them freely and give them often. Leave something everywhere you go and with everyone you meet. Keep it simple so you can keep it up.

Physical Touch—Proceed with great caution on this one. No need to spur a sexual harassment lawsuit. You can, however, touch targets easily and safely with strong handshakes, direct eye contact, and of course handwritten notes, phone calls, mail, and e-mails. Communication of any kind counts, though the more direct it is, the bigger it rates. Communicate regularly with targets and make it personal.

Final Word on Emotions

Emotions are powerful. They are triggers and they are deciders. They bring people together and they tear them apart.

To be an effective marketer, you must stir emotions in everything you do internally and in every message you send externally. You must stir the right emotions, the ones that matter to your target audience. And, you must stir them constantly. People remember and talk about the emotions they always or never feel. They share stories about what makes them feel really good or really bad or really anything.

Once again, consistency comes into play. Mixed messages and inconsistent behaviors only take targets on emotional roller coasters and that's never good. If someone recommends a particular restaurant to a friend, and that restaurant has a "bad night," his judgment becomes questioned and the whole marketing cycle comes to a halt.

Whatever emotion is important to your targets, make them feel it in a big way every time in everything you do.

Stir Mindfulness

Most of your external marketing time and effort will be devoted to stirring mindfulness. This means that targets think of you first when they want, need, or otherwise consider what you offer. Remember, the only way to ensure that you are there when targets need you is to be there all the time. Prospects and customers must never be allowed to forget you. They must bump into you constantly. Everywhere they turn and every time they turn around, you must not-so-humbly remind them that you exist and why you are a smart choice for them. To make these encounters more productive, your message must be consistent in how it looks and what it says. With a quick glance or little snippet, targets must be able to identify you, and better yet, know what you have to say. Of course the greater the emotional charge of those efforts, the more successful they will be.

Stir Conviction

It can take some work to make a customer firm in his belief that you are his best choice. If you are a restaurant, you want to be your customer's favorite restaurant. If you are a hair salon, you want customers who are willing to wait a few extra days to get an appointment. If you are a business-to-business service provider, you want your customers to declare that they wouldn't do business with anyone else. That's conviction, and that's always your goal. The quickest way to earn conviction once you earn a customer is to do a superb job of delivering and taking care of that customer—in a way that is meaningful to him. That's an essential point here. What you think is good is only as good as your customer thinks it is. Everything must be viewed and orchestrated from the customer's perspective. Remember, marketing isn't all about you.

To stir conviction, you will need to constantly answer the two major questions all targets ask:

What's in It for Me?

As a customer yourself, isn't that what you want to know? Most people understand the importance of this question, but if you look around, far fewer are answering it. Customers want to know what's in it for them. They will demand an answer, and you had better be ready to give them one. If you were asked right now to tell someone what's in it for your customer to do business with you, what would you say? Would you be clear, assured, and poignant in your answer, or would you stammer with a muddled mishmash of marketing babble? You must know, in no uncertain terms, why customers should choose you. If you are to be an effective marketer, you can't just go around telling targets how great you are because, frankly, they don't care. They just want to know what's in it for them. They want to know why they should trust you, pay you, talk to you, listen to you. If you want to lead customers to a state of conviction where they step up with a resounding YES, then you have to tell them what's in it for them. Are you?

What Have You Done for Me Lately?

Current customers want to know what you've done for them lately. If they aren't sure, they are more likely to answer the mating call of your competitors. Keeping customers out of complacency must be a standing focus of your marketing. Complacency is congestion in the making, and you never know what or who else could sweep a customer off her feet if you aren't paying attention—and giving her attention. I'm sure you understand the dangers, but I'll ask you to honestly assess if you are guilty of forgetting about your customers while you chase more fish.

Customers need to be constantly courted and emotionally connected. They must be forever mindful of what you do for them and what else you can do for them. Put the love languages to work. Keep communications open and personal, and take the lead. Contact customers just to say hello and ask how they're doing. Check in after an order to make sure everything was done properly. Tell them about your new equipment or the new staff you hired to help them. Tell them what you do for them behind the scenes. And of course, tell them thank you.

Lead your customers to seeing you as their partner, resource, and friend. Tell your customers what you've done for them lately and do it often.

Where Are You Taking Me?

In addition to those two pivotal questions, business-to-business customers also want to know, *Where are you taking me?* Customers want to work with people and companies who will make them better—who will give them a competitive edge, keep them apprised of market trends, and lead them to the next best thing. They want relationships that will benefit them in the future as well as the present. If targets know they can count on you to lead them where they need to go (even if that place doesn't exist yet), then they will eagerly jump on your train and stay. Where are you taking your customers? Tell them.

Stir Word-of-Mouth

If you want people to talk about you, you have to give them something to talk about. We all know the power of word-of-mouth, so get those mouths buzzing in a good way. Do something in such an unusual or extraordinary manner that customers can't help but tell others about it. Make the experience of working with you so wonderful, so different, that customers have to pass the news to their associates and online community. Today, a little whisper can become a raging roar with the viral assistance of the Internet. It doesn't take something earth-shattering to get people talking either.

I tell people all the time about my friends at the neighborhood post office. First, how often do we call our postal workers friends? Well, these guys have made themselves friends, not by what they do, but how they do it. The experience is always the same. They smile at me when I enter, and some even know my name. Everyone there is always cordial, professional, and eager to help. They have obvious protocols to make sure patrons get through quickly and hassle-free, even when they're lined up out the door. Those attributes may seem small and insignificant, but collectively they make a big impression. Compared to this office, my experience with any other always falls short, sometimes shamefully so. I will actually hold mail until I can personally bring it to my postal pals even though there's a box right outside my door. For some not-so-logical reason, I just feel safer entrusting my important business to the professionals at this particular center. That's enough for me to go out of my way to go there. I'm definitely a customer of conviction, and because I have such strong feelings about them, I talk a lot about them to my friends and neighbors.

What are you giving your targets to talk about?

Get Stirring

Nothing happens until there's motion. If you aren't constantly stirring the pot in your business, you're asking for trouble. Keep your business flowing by stirring awareness, emotions, mindfulness, conviction, and word-of-mouth. Stir them in each letter you write, every e-mail you send, every presentation you give, and in everything you do everyday in the normal operation of your business. Every time you pick up a spoon to stir your gumbo, soup, coffee, or tea, ask yourself:

What am I doing to stir the pot in my business today?

What am I doing to turn oblivious bystanders into committed customers who will spread great word-of-mouth about my business?

You know what to do now. You have sound direction to guide you in every marketing endeavor and in every step you take every day. You can't lose. Just start stirring and keep stirring!

Something to Think About

▶ What pots do you need to stir in your marketing?

▶ Are you consistently and constantly stirring awareness, emotions, mindfulness, conviction, and word-of-mouth?

▶ What emotions matter most to each of your target groups? How can you stir those feelings inside your business in and your external promotions?

▶ Are you telling your customers what's in it for them, what you've done for them lately, and where you're taking them?

▶ Are you giving your marketing time to work (at least seven to nine contacts to hit their radar)?

▶ How can you show customers that you love them?

▶ What do customers have to say about you right now? Do you need to give them something new to talk about?

Tips 11–25
on How to Put Your Marketing Into Action

11. **Say it once, say it 52 times.** The average person is estimated to have at least 52 people in his circle of influence—people he lives with, is related to, works with, socializes with, and could otherwise impact the opinion of. That means when you make an impression on one person, it could be quickly and easily spread to at least 52 other people who would take the message seriously. News travels fast. Whether it's another 52 people or hundreds of thousands reached virally online, every impression you make is likely to be multiplied. Give people something great to spread around.

12. **What's the price? What's the value?** When the perception of value is greater than the perception of cost, your customer will buy happily. Even though price is a common objection, it's not always the reason for not buying or choosing (as long as you're targeting an audience that really does have the capacity to pay). The secret is to first understand what matters to your customer. Then help the target understand your product or service in terms of that value. If you're getting the price objection, consider it your cue to dig deeper with more questions about what is really important to your target.

13. **Treat your vendors well.** They play a critical role in your success and your sanity. Show your appreciation. Say thank you with a note, small gift, or big referral. Make working with you pleasant and profitable for them. The better you take care of your vendors, the better they'll take care of you. Plus, vendors are usually in a position to direct business your way, giving you all the more incentive to treat them well. Make vendor appreciation part of your marketing strategy.

14. **Share love and gratitude with customers.** At least once a year, send customers a card or special note for the sole purpose of expressing gratitude. Give them a heartfelt message that goes beyond, "Thank you for making us successful." Make it about them and include no marketing or

sales language whatsoever. Don't forget about Valentine's Day either. It's always a good idea to tell your customers you love them.

15. **Give a little lagniappe.** *Lagniappe* (lan yap) is a French word used and loved by Cajuns like me to mean "a little something extra." It's the cherry on the chocolate sundae and the prize in the cereal box. It makes great impressions and makes you memorable, so throw some in all of your pots. Your targets will love you for it.

16. **Make your buyer a hero in his own company.** No man is an island, and how you serve your customer impacts his standing and relationships with his customers, peers, and managers. If you don't come through for him, you make him look bad. Always consider your customer's personal perspective and how you can bolster his image in his world. Make customers look really smart for choosing you, and you'll have many more choosing you.

17. **Make their entire company love you.** Want to really win over a company? Buy lunch for its entire staff. Send cake, cookies, or other treats for everyone to share—not just one representative or department.

18. **What's your "warm fuzzy" factor?** People buy from people they like, so be likeable. If customers aren't feeling the love, they will likely search another option. Build a great "warm fuzzy factor" by showing appreciation, courtesy, and genuine concern for others' happiness, comfort, convenience, confidence, security, ease, and whatever else matters to them. Notes, gifts, fun surprises, food, a good handshake, warm welcome, or attentive ear might be all it takes to score big points, but you'll have to be consistent for it to be meaningful. Make warm fuzzies part of your culture and your character.

19. **Tell customers when you do something extra.** In life, it's well and right to give without attachment, but in business, it's important that customers know what you do for them. If you give a customer something at no charge, tell her. If you throw in some extra quantities or give him a discount, tell him. You don't need to be overly boastful about it, but you do need to make customers aware of all the value they get from your company. If they can't see it directly, they won't know unless you tell them.

20. **No matter what you sell, you are providing a tangible and intangible.** An appliance store may sell machines, but customers are really buying the intangible benefit those machines can provide for them. An accounting firm may offer consulting and intelligence, but customers also

need tangible tax returns and money saved. Whether you are a product supplier or service provider, you deliver both a tangible and an intangible offering. Get clear on what each is for you and promote both of them.

21. **Ask for referrals.** Customers always know someone they can refer to you, but they may need a little prodding to do it. Ask for referrals and you'll get them. Don't ask and you likely won't. Consider incorporating a tool into your service cycle to ask for referrals. Give people an incentive to give them to you, and definitely send a huge thank you to those who do. The more you reward, the more you get.

22. **Engage all of their senses.** The more senses you engage in your targets, the more meaningful and memorable the connection. Make targets participate in some way. Make them stick something, check something, create something. Give them things to touch and feel like bulky packages and interesting paper textures. Use colors that provoke the right psychological effect. Use striking images of people in the emotions you want them to have or that you can help them lose. Engage them so they'll engage you.

23. **Make your office smell really good.** Aromatherapy isn't just for the spa. Our olfactory sense is extremely powerful and connected to our brain's memory function, so tap into the power of the nose. Give targets a pleasant aromatic surprise when they enter your business. Put them in the right state-of-mind with soothing lavender, stimulating citrus, or calming chamomile. The sense of smell is an underutilized asset in the business world, but it's another part of the experience of working with you. Give people something to sniff about!

24. **Get everyone in the mood with music.** Music can quickly and powerfully set the tone for anything. Play it throughout your facility, during telephone hold time, and at events. Open and close company meetings with it. Make music a staple in your tool chest to crank up the energy, mellow the mood, or add spice to any gathering, large or small.

25. **Think about what your customer doesn't want.** Of course you need to know what your customer wants, but you also need to address what he doesn't want. There are obvious things such as ignorance and rudeness, but dig deeper. Get to the details like long wait times, too much paperwork, or feeling like the proverbial herd of cattle. Establish controls to avoid these frustrations in your business and then boldly market that you're paying attention and that you're different.

Standing Out From the Crowd, the Clutter, and the Competition

Getting out of the gray.

Chapter 6

How Do You Stand Out?

Getting clear on how you need to get noticed

It's mighty noisy out there! The marketplace is rampant and over-cluttered with people trying to get your attention. With all that noise, it's hard to hear anything at all. More than ever, we marketers are called to be distinctive, to stand out in an over-crowded, hypercompetitive world. In fact, it's absolutely mandatory.

Predictable, ho-hum messages will be caught in the global recycle bin of misguided marketing. The formula of telling everybody how great you are with your state-of-the art solutions, commitment to customer service, and the best prices in town just won't cut it. Everyone will see right through you—if they see you at all. It's going to take more if you want to get noticed and get attention. It's going to take conscious, deliberate action to stand out from the crowd, the clutter, and the competition.

First, you must build a company that stands out. Then you have to create marketing that stands out so you can promote your standout company. Finally, you have to make sure everyone is standing out on the same page.

Certainly there are many ways to stand out, though not all of them favorable. You could run naked in the street or punch a customer in the nose. That would make you stand out in the next morning's headlines, but you probably wouldn't do much good for your business.

It is easy to point to countless examples of rudeness, negligence, malpractice, dysfunction, ignorance, and utter foolishness that pervade the marketplace and attack us at every turn as customers. Indeed those perpetrators stand out, and from them we learn an all-important lesson: It is not just required *that* we stand out, but that we stand out in a way *that serves us*. That's going to take some thinking.

There are essentially four ways to stand out in a meaningful marketing manner, and I will give you full disclosure shortly. First, we need to lay out the mindsets that make them work.

You Already Do Stand Out

The notion of standing out makes some people uneasy. They don't enjoy the spotlight. They prefer to be hidden behind the scenes and in the shadows. Well, if that's you, here's a news flash. That behavior won't help you be an effective marketer. Plus, whether you know it or not and whether you like it or not, you already do stand out. There's no escaping it. If you're living and breathing, you're standing out in some way, likely many ways. The only question is whether you're standing out in a way that will serve you.

If I were to ask your friends what comes to mind when they think of you, what do you think they would say? You know they would all have an answer! What if I asked your spouse, partner, child, parent, coworker, boss, associate, or neighbor? What adjectives would they use to describe you? What words would be at the top of their head and tip of their tongue? And, most importantly, would you like what they said?

Let's turn the tables. What would you say if I asked you to describe your spouse or best friend? What about your favorite customer? What adjectives would you use to characterize that person or company to someone else? Why are those particular words at the top of your mind?

Now let's look at your business. If we asked your customers to share what comes to mind when they think of you, what would they say? What if we asked your employees or coworkers, vendors, associates, a stranger off the street? What adjectives would each group likely use? Would you get a common answer or varied responses? Would you like what you heard? Would their perception of you be accurate? Would it be complete? Would their impressions further your relationship and help you achieve your marketing and business goals?

Of course the hope is that they all have favorable things to say. But, even if their comments are complimentary, they may not be beneficial. Standing out from a marketing perspective means not just making a positive impression, but making the right impression.

For example, my friends may describe me as a "pleasant person." That's wonderful. I definitely want to be considered pleasant versus unpleasant, but with business prospects, I need them thinking something more substantial and relative to my skills and offerings. Being perceived as pleasant alone isn't enough to make great things happen in my business. I want my targets to readily see me as an expert. I want them to say, "Oh, she's that 'stir the pot' lady who makes marketing practical and is a great speaker and trainer." If I can stand out like that, then I can definitely attract good business to my company. That means all of my marketing must be strategically geared toward creating this reaction, this impression and perception.

Getting Clear on How You Stand Out

Asking poignant and self-illuminating questions such as, *How do people perceive me?* awakens us to the impact and importance of our daily habits and tendencies. It also arms us with the information and clarity we need to stand out in a way that helps us succeed.

How we stand out must never be left to happenstance. Like all of our marketing, we must take charge of orchestrating the circumstances that will convey correct and complete messages about us. We must be mindful and strategic in how we stand out in order to propel our success. In all ways, we must be truthful. We must be authentic. And, by all means, we must make the right story shine through.

Marketers spend inordinate amounts of time laboring over messages for print communications, advertising campaigns, and every other promotion—as we should. But those aren't the only messages that must be kneaded and molded. What we do and how we act in the unassuming minutiae of business and life become either constant whispers or bold blarings to the marketplace. Either way, they become attached to us in the conscious and unconscious minds of our targets. It is inevitable and unavoidable. We all stand out in some way whether we know it or not and whether we like it or not. The big question is how. How do we stand out now, and how do we need to stand out to help us accomplish our goals?

As marketers, we can say anything we want "out there," but those messages are not the only ones heard and registered. Everything else about us goes into the music mix that is our business and our reputation. We will either sing in harmony or we'll throw a

> *We all stand out in some way whether we know it or not and whether we like it or not. The big question is how. How do we stand out now, and how do we need to stand out to help us accomplish our goals?*

bunch of scatter-brained messages to the crowd, adding only more noise. That's certainly not the making of a marketing machine, but it is what I commonly find in the marketplace.

I find that most people stagger through life and business completely oblivious and unconcerned about the impact of their day-to-day actions. They go about their daily barrage of to-do lists, e-mail checks, conference calls, social networking, fire fighting, and paper pushing without realizing that their words, actions, attitudes, habits, quirks, idiosyncrasies, traits, and virtues become their individual stories. It's true for all of us. What we do and how we do it every day is what our story becomes. Our individual stories merge to form the collective tale of our companies that then gets circulated and archived as such. It either serves us or it doesn't. It helps the marketplace to understand who we are, or it makes it further confused.

Marketers think about these things. They are mindful of how their target audiences could perceive them at all times. "Perception control" is always on duty because targets are constantly processing impressions and formulating perceptions that impact whether or not they do what our marketing asks them to do.

If you are to stand out from the crowd, the clutter, and the competition—as you must—then you must step up from the apathetic drone of the daily chores of life and business. "Keeping it all together" is not good enough if you want to be a standout company and a marketing machine. As a marketer, you must mastermind everything and leave nothing to chance. You must make great and consistent impressions. You must take conscious and deliberate action to stand out and stand out in the right way.

Your Customers Want You to Stand Out

If you offer a product or service that is meaningful and valuable to your target audience, they want to know about it. If you provide an extraordinary experience in how you deliver an ordinary product or service, they want to know about it. They might not be ready to buy, or care to hear about it all the time, but if you are clear on who your target audience is and what is important to them, then it is just a matter of time and repetition before you make a connection. You just have to keep stirring.

As customers, we like working with people and companies who are special in some way. It stirs our emotions, boosts our egos, and makes us feel smart. It gives us a great story to tell, almost as if we discovered some buried treasure.

So why then would you ever be shy about standing out? Getting noticed and getting attention isn't just for you. Your marketplace wants it. And isn't the core purpose of any business to give the marketplace what it wants and is willing to pay for?

There's a wonderful Yiddish adage that proclaims, "We're all crazy good at something." When you deliver "crazy good" to the marketplace, it does and will take notice. So be crazy good at what you do and how you do it. Be crazy good at making great impressions. Be crazy good at stirring the pot.

When you are crazy good in any way, you will stand out and your targets will thank you for it. In fact, you aren't being fair if you don't. If you can make a valuable contribution to the lives of your targets—if you can help them shine and thrive in their world—then you are doing them a disservice by keeping your contributions to yourself. Your targets want you to stand out, and they will reward you well for it.

In marketing, there is no room for quiet and shy. If you are not excited and passionate enough about what you do to tell everyone about it, then maybe you need to consider a career change. If you are not motivated to make your business crazy good, extraordinary, or special in some way, then you should not be surprised when your results are crazy bland, ordinary, and nothing to cheer about.

It's time to step up and stand out in a way that serves you and others. As said by the beloved Nelson Mandela, "Your playing small does not serve the world. Who are you not to be great?"

Taking Your Stand

So now that it is clear that you must stand out, that you already do stand out, and that you must take charge to stand out not only in a favorable way, but in the right way, let's put these bits of wisdom into practice.

For this, we'll need another practical definition to work from. As I see it, standing out for outstanding results in life and business encompasses three things:

1. Getting noticed.

2. Getting attention.

3. Achieving your desired results.

To reach standing out victory, you must be successful on all three fronts. First you must break and shine through the clutter so people simply know you exist. Then you must get them engaged and participating where they will at least read, listen, and give time and thought to your message. Finally, there's the ultimate, determining step—motivating targets to act, call, consider, click, visit, listen, answer, trust, buy, buy more, buy again, and generally do whatever helps you reach your objectives.

Most likely you are working hard to get noticed and get attention, maybe even harder than you have to. That will come more easily as you learn the four keys to standing out. In the end, it is all about achieving your desired results, and that means getting crystal clear on what those are.

For specific marketing initiatives, desired results will be straightforward. Turn prospects into customers. Make current customers better customers. But before those things can happen, you must go back to the adjectives of how you want people to readily perceive and describe you. The expectation is that, if targets readily perceive you in the right way, they will want to do business with you. It's not complicated, but we make it so when we jump into marketing without pre-thinking what we want and how we need to position ourselves to get there.

So let's think about adjectives and descriptions. How do you want targets to describe you to others? Expert? Easy and convenient? Fun company to work with? Environmentally conscious? Industry leader? Dependable? Innovative? Cost-smart? Unique experience? Whatever it is, you need to decide. Just like determining the emotions that matter to your target, you need to clarify the adjectives that can help you direct your internal and external marketing in a meaningful way.

The results you seek from one target group may differ from those of another, so consider all of your "pots." My list for how I want to be perceived by customers is different than the list I use for my children or my friends or staff. There is usually some overlap, but there is no single list. Our relationships are too varied and complex.

Give careful forethought to how you must stand out with each of your target groups to make sure you're standing out in the right way to get noticed, get attention, and most importantly, achieve your desired results.

Chapter 7

Getting Your Image and Identity in Sync

Preparing to stand out

Standout companies and standout marketers have cohesive messages. They know who they are. Everyone else knows who they are. It's easy to decipher because there is no ambiguity. Everything that is them and everything that represents them is made of the same mass. What's on the inside reflects what's on the outside and vice versa. These companies are the epitome of consistency and the raciest of marketing machines.

That is your ultimate desired result—for your external and internal personas to be one—and it is completely doable. You will need to shed yourself of that looming hodgepodge of scatter-brained messages and mixed customer experiences, but you can do it. You must do it. You must stand out and in the right way. Your target market demands it, and your success depends on it.

This alignment of internal and external forces is called getting your image and identity in sync. It is the moment when everything that is you and everything that represents you converge into a single, coherent form—kind of like when oil and flour become a workable roux.

Your image is what lives on the outside. It's what others perceive of you. Your identity is who you really are on the inside—your skills, talents, attributes, weaknesses, strengths, virtues, and general offering to the world. To be successful, your image and identity must be in sync at all times. When they are, that's authenticity and the making of a brand. When they aren't, you're either overselling yourself and essentially lying to the marketplace, or you're underselling yourself and missing tons of marketing opportunities.

We all know those companies who talk a good talk on the outside, but when we give them a chance or become their customer, we get less than promised. We feel cheated and angry. On the flip side, there are tons of great businesses that lay low on marketing and miss profuse opportunities to tout their offerings. I chuckle quietly when I hear companies boast how they are "the best-kept secret in town." It sounds good, but it's hard to stand out when you're a secret.

A simplified way to think about image and identity is a plate of food. True chefs will tell you that presentation is key. Some would say everything. "People eat with their eyes first," they proclaim.

Undoubtedly, the more appealing food looks, the more people will want to eat it. In that case, it has a good image, but what about its identity? The first bite is the tell-all. If the dish tastes as good as it looks, it has delivered on its visual promise. If it doesn't, it has misrepresented itself to the taster.

In contrast, a dish may not look too appetizing on the plate, but despite its questionable appearance, its flavors will send taste buds singing—if you can get anyone to try it. Its identity is strong, but it has nothing working for it on the outside to reel in the takers.

The perfect meal is one that looks great and tastes just as great. Same with your business. You need equally strong outer appearances and internal substance. You need complete alignment with the outside and the inside. That is having your image and identity in sync.

Lining Things Up

As you would guess, it takes conscious, deliberate action and constant tending to maintain synchronicity between your image and identity. But let's not over-dramatize the issue. Keeping your image and identity in sync should not be complicated if you are clear on who you are, and you're willing to speak up about it.

Part of it is just decision-making. You get to choose who you are and who you want to be as long as you get the approval of your target audience. Then it's just a matter of congruency. Every single atom of your company's existence must be calibrated to that decision about who you want to be, creating an authentic match between your internal and external personas.

Why would that be so difficult? If you are a serious person, you tend to attract serious people and produce serious material. If you are funny, you attract funny people and produce funny material. That's an oversimplification of course, but no need to make things overly difficult. When you decide who you are, there is an inherent set of rules that comes with that choice. All things that match should be let in and embraced. All things that don't should be stiff-armed and avoided.

Think about designing a room. Going into the project, the designer works with the owner to determine the style of design—traditional, modern, rustic, whatever. Then it is the designer's job to add in and edit out whatever makes that room the design of choice. The designer establishes a color palette. When the palette is adhered to, the room is visually pleasing and coordinated, but throw in an uncomplimentary hue, and the whole look is wrecked.

The same goes for your business. You must decide what you want to be and then be it all the way. Everything else must be edited out. It's a simple yes/no scorecard. Everything either helps or hurts, is consistent or inconsistent. Everything either creates circulation or congestion. All of that "indifferent" we talked about in Phase 1 is a just a bunch of gunky build-up in your marketing machine. Either you repurpose it into something great or you eliminate it.

You cannot be a standout company unless and until your internal and external personas are mirror reflections. Without that, you will work far harder and spend far more money in your marketing to earn far less.

Consequences of Misalignment

It is always easy to spot those companies who get their image and identity out of sync. They are the ones flying by the seat of their pants and changing course every other week. They blow wherever the wind or latest craze carries them. They are consumed with false starts and unhappy endings. We as customers see the side effects and become victims of their inconsistent performance.

Sometimes companies are allowed to get away with such messiness. The only milk supplier for 50 miles can likely do whatever it pleases. Still, it is a mindset more than a circumstance. Personally, even if I could get away with multiple personalities, I wouldn't try it. I have great pride in my business and the contribution I make. I know the impact of what I do every day is far greater than I could ever know. I choose to be a great company and a mindful marketer.

Companies who thrive, and suffer less in stressful times, are the ones who remain firm in who they are, and who proudly and profusely tell their story.

They don't need to be liked or loved by everyone, just the targets who are right for them. They know who their ideal targets are because they have taken the time to identify them. They understand what is important to them and they act accordingly. If these companies must change their identity in any way, their image changes with it. What's on the outside always moves in step with the inside. The story told is the story read. What you see is always what you get—even when it's something new or different.

Companies who operate this way are also easily spotted, but for the right reasons. For me, Southwest Airlines is always a bright example. Southwest Airlines is crystal clear about who they are and what they offer, which is far more than an airplane ride. It's a friendly travel experience. They know their audience and they cater to it like a mother to a child, as long as it remains in line with their mission. Ask anyone in the United States about Southwest Airlines and you'll find many common descriptions such as convenient, friendly, spirited, cost-effective, and fun. Those things shine through in everything the company does.

Look at the playfulness of their external marketing and of their staff. They make me laugh every time I fly, giving me a welcome break from the stresses of travel. They are quick to tell customers like me how much they LUV us and they aren't afraid to show it. Experience their company online, in person, and in the air and you'll feel the LUV there, too. It's obvious that their people LUV working there, and that makes the flying experience for the rest of us very LUVable.

The Southwest message is clear, consistent, and repetitious, as all good marketing should be. This alignment has propelled their success and made them the airline of choice for hundreds of thousands of flyers including myself. They are indeed one of the best case studies and propositions for keeping your image and identity in sync. They deserve every bit of their success.

Now let's bring the topic down about 40,000 feet. If you are to stand out in a successful way, you must be just as unabashed in being and promoting who you decide to be. That means communicating a clear vision throughout your company. That means paying attention to every detail and editing out anything that doesn't fit, even if it's a customer. That means saying no when you need to say no.

I learned this all too-important lesson early in my career. I was asked by an organization to develop and deliver sexual harassment prevention courses to their members. As a professional speaker, I love any chance to get in front of an audience. I took the assignment because it was easy, because I liked the people involved and, odd to say, because I thought it would be fun. Until reality hit me over the head, that is.

One day after the presentation, a lady came up to me wanting to share her story. She had real emotional trauma over something that was happening in her workplace. I was really disturbed. Shortly after, a man asked me to help him organize the notes he was preparing for his lawyer in defense of harassment charges made against him. Right then I knew that I was standing in a place I didn't belong. I was there as a speaker, totally disconnected to my topic and the impact it had on others. I needed to either dedicate myself to the cause or get out. Marketing professionals do not need to be giving sexual harassment training no matter how well they can deliver a program. Clearly I had allowed my image and identity to get terribly out of sync.

When you work blindly and allow your business to run on wind and whim, you end up in places you don't need to be and with people you don't need to be working with. Get clear on who you are, who you serve, and what makes you and your target audience a good fit. It will make your marketing so much easier and wildly more successful.

Want to Buy a Car?

What you see is definitely not always what you get. Let's look at a lighter example of image and identity out of kilter. When I mention the stereotypical Hollywood used car salesman, what images come to mind? Likely you envision a plaid jacket, polyester pants, bad hair, greasy smile, and of course lots of gold jewelry. That may be a bit over the top, but it certainly speaks to the perceptions we have about this presumably shady character. Now think about a luxury car salesman. The image is quite different: slick suit, perfect shave and haircut, spit-shined shoes. A stark contrast from his non-professional counterpart.

But, when we boil it all down, does any of that really tell us how well these specimens can sell? The outer appearance and image of the used car salesman makes him questionable, so we may never give him a chance to demonstrate his abilities. If he's a great salesperson with a reputable product, then we both lose. He loses the sale, and we lose the opportunity because we were too turned off to give him a try. In contrast, the image of the luxury car salesman makes him highly approachable, giving him the opportunity to showcase his talents and wares. If he proves instead to be arrogant, incompetent, or non-responsive, or his product less than perceived, then he loses the business, and we leave feeling frustrated and deceived. We call "those guys" idiots and never return to the dealership.

Every day all types of companies suffer cost and consequence by having their image and identity out of sync. Let's make sure that's never you. Time to align your marketing machine.

Dimensions of Identity

Your image is the culmination of messages consciously placed in the marketplace by you, your customers, your competition, the media, and everyone else who has something to say about you. Until targets personally experience your company, they will form their opinions, judgments, and perceptions about you based on what they see and hear from the outside. Your own message must drown out all others.

With identity, there are three dimensions to be considered as you define who you are and how you need to stand out in your marketplace:

1. **Identity as *viewed* by the target:**

    These are first impressions made at first glance into your company. What does the target perceive of you by what she sees when she peeks into your business?

2. **Identity as *experienced* by the target:**

    This is what your target encounters once she steps inside your company as an active prospect or customer and once she begins interacting with your people and processes. Is the experience of working with you consistent with what you promised on the outside and how it appeared looking in? Do you back up your marketing claims? Are you really what you say you are?

3. **Identity as *proclaimed* by the target:**

    This is the story targets will share about you to the marketplace after they register all of those impressions and experiences. How consistent will their story be with your message? Have you given your targets something great to talk about? Can they relate to your story easily?

When all of these elements are perfectly aligned, your company becomes one voice and one face in the marketplace—someone targets can understand, rely on, and easily refer to others.

Image and Identity Gone Bad

Look around anywhere, everywhere, and you'll find plenty examples of image and identity gone bad. Sometimes it is so explicitly obvious that you just shake your head and ask yourself, *How could they not get this?* All the time I am amazed at the silliness and sometimes utter stupidity that runs amuck in businesses that say they want to be successful.

How many times have we entered the elevator in a beautiful hotel lobby only to be dropped off in a dark, drab hallway that felt like a slum alley? What are those people thinking? Do they not think we notice? Or don't care? Those companies like to put on a good show, but their identity is terribly out of whack.

A similar example involves a high-end, reputable furniture store where I was extremely excited to spend a few thousand dollars to make my bedroom look as dazzling as their floor display. Except, when I went to hand over my hard-earned money, I dropped my jaw. I was lead to the back of the store where I felt like I had walked into the previous hotel hallway. Suddenly, the floors changed from comforting carpet to ugly, cold tile. The walls weren't bold and colorful, but boring beige with lots of scrapes and smudges. The furniture obviously wasn't from their own inventory, but instead cheap make-do's from the local office supply store. There were tacky notes on the walls and an overall sense of "we don't care." How surprising. How terribly disappointing. Talk about bad impressions when great impressions could have been so easily made. I'm guessing they could have gotten some great deals on some good furniture. And how much extra would it have really cost to carpet the small area where they bring customers at the most significant point of the sales cycle, the moment they actually pay you? Whatever the cost, it would have been worth twenty times the money. Amazing! What are those people thinking?

When I see companies take shortcuts like this, I know there is more mud lurking about their business. Reality taints their shiny marketing messages, and I become skeptical. All of their hard work to win me over is essentially lost as I leave in distaste.

As marketers, we must maintain a keen awareness of the good, the bad, and the ugly of marketing that exists all around us. Pay attention to what impresses you and what you find irritating or displeasing. If it impacts you, it's likely to impact your target audience. There is indeed much to be learned about marketing everywhere you go.

How Companies Get Their Image and Identity Out of Sync

- Try to be too many things to too many people.
- Don't get clear on how they want or need to stand out in the marketplace to achieve their desired results.
- Don't market themselves aggressively.
- Don't do what they promise.
- Constantly change their story about who they are.
- Dress and present their company sloppily or inconsistently with the way they wish to be perceived.
- Use poorly produced materials while claiming they stand for high quality and high standards.
- Don't portray the person or company they say they are in print.
- Don't establish the daily habits to stand out in the right way.

Chapter 8

Who Are You Anyway?

Getting clear on how you need to be perceived

Getting your image and identity in sync begins with some or all of your team sitting around a table in front of a writing board. If you are a solo entrepreneur, you may want to recruit a trusted friend or advisor to help you get an unbiased perspective of your business. Together you will need to mastermind a few guiding precepts for how you operate and market your business every day.

To be a company in complete marketing alignment, you must achieve and maintain mastery of each of these five steps:

1. Clarify your vision of how you want to be perceived by others.

2. Identify the adjectives, characteristics, attributes, and actions that go with your vision (List of Attributes).

3. Objectively assess where you are in relation to your goal.

4. Develop a plan to consistently act, interact, and communicate in a way that is consistent with your vision and defined attributes.

5. Hold yourself accountable to your established standards.

Your List of Attributes

To ensure that you stand out in the right way, in a way that serves you, you will need to define, commit to paper, and firmly establish what I call your List of Attributes. This outlines the specific adjectives that describe how you need to be perceived in the marketplace through your image and how you must behave to establish your congruent identity. These will become the values and characteristics that are to drive everything you do internally and externally. They are what you will work to instill in the mind and voices of your targets through what they see and experience. They are the adjectives you would want targets to use to describe you to others.

This is conscious, deliberate marketing in action. And, as with everything else, you will want to recruit the insights and input of everyone in your company. After all, the identity of the company is the collective identity of its individuals. You will need everyone thinking, acting, and communicating in sync with your List of Attributes. Of course you will also need to apply the list when hiring new members for your team.

On the List of Attributes for my company, Sonnier Marketing, we have adjectives and descriptions such as creative, inspiring, difference-makers, thoughtful, accurate, driven, reliable, responsive, practical, expert, and fun. This list becomes the benchmark by which we base our decisions, make choices, and assess everything that is us and everything that represents us. Yours can take whatever form works for you and your target audience.

Once you have made your official List of Attributes, you will need to have extensive dialog with your team to simply ask and answer, *What does this mean for the customer?* If your list includes the adjective "reliable," for example, then you would list all of the things that would make a customer perceive you as reliable, such as: always answers the telephone by the third ring; always returns telephone calls and e-mails the same day received; always produces price estimates within 24 hours; staff members always follow through on promises; and, the company institutes an extra quality control protocol to ensure jobs are accurately produced to specification.

As you detail each of your adjectives, you may discover the need for additional systems, processes, or tools. That's exactly what this exercise is intended to do—to make you a better company. And don't be shy about it. Making improvements in your business gives you something new to market. As within, so without.

Time to Decide

▸ What is your vision for your company? How to do you want and need to be perceived by your targets?

▸ What are the characteristics, attributes, and actions that go with making your vision happen?

▸ What message do you need to send in your external marketing?

▶ Where do you stand right now in relation to your goal?

▶ What are you currently relating that is possibly telling a bad, indifferent, wrong, or incomplete story about you?

▶ What do you need to do to get your image and identity perfectly aligned?

■

AreYour Image and Identity in Sync?

Take the Quiz!

So, where do *you* stand with your image and identity? Take this simple quiz by answering true or false to the following questions. You can take it from a personal or company perspective, or both.

T F 1. I like the way I present myself to the world.

T F 2. Those who know me would describe me as a "what you see is what you get" kind of person (or company or organization).

T F 3. I would describe myself as a "what you see is what you get" kind of person (or company or organization).

T F 4. The way I dress and physically present myself to the outside world accurately reflects how I want to be perceived.

T F 5. I generally behave the same all the time, regardless of whom I'm around.

T F 6. The way people would describe the materials I use to represent myself (business card, brochure, and so on) is the same way they would describe me personally.

T F 7. I take charge of telling the marketplace what they need to know about me to achieve my goals.

T F 8. Everything I say about myself is true.

T F 9. It is easy for others to see what values and traits are important to me.

T F 10. I am seldom surprised about what others say or think of me.

T F 11. My prospects are clear on what I offer, and they can effectively refer business to me.

T F 12. I always do what I say I'm going to do.

T F 13. I feel like I live and do business authentically.

If you answered true to 11 or more statements, congratulations! Your image and identity are likely in good sync and you're well positioned for effective marketing.

If you answered true to 8-10 statements, you're doing a good job, but have a few areas to focus on. Identify them and make some adjustments in the way you're presenting yourself or in the way you're standing behind your marketing claims.

If you answered true to 7 or fewer statements, it's time to identify where there is a disconnect and what you can do to fix it. You're likely missing opportunities and struggling somewhere unnecessarily.

Whatever your score, carefully consider how you can turn any statement answered false into true. What adjustments do you need to make in the way you think, act, and communicate to make this area work positively for you? Getting your image and identity in sync isn't always easy, but it's absolutely necessary if you want to communicate a correct and complete story about who you are, what you can do, and what you can offer others. More doors will open for you and you'll find that success flows all the more quickly!

Chapter 9

Time to Stand Out

Go from ordinary to extraordinary

With clarity about your goals, your image, and your identity, you stand ready to stand out—in the right way, in a way that will serve you. You're ready to get noticed, get attention, and achieve your desired results.

Get Out of the Gray

Most individuals and businesses live and operate in what I call the gray zone. That is that big gray ball where the masses travel. It's where everyone looks, sounds, and acts like everyone else, because it's safe and it's comfortable. It's also the so-what-nothing-special-be-like-everybody-else zone. It's void of creativity and individuality. It's how everybody looks. What everybody says and how they say it. What everyone does and how they do it. It's where standing out is impossible.

You can't stand out if you look, sound, and act like everyone else. You can't distinguish yourself from the competition. You can't be the best or the most desired. You can't win like you want to win, and you can't make marketing as easy as it could be.

To stand out, you have to want to be extraordinary and you have to be willing to step out of the gray. No more conforming. No more safety net "because everyone else is do-

ing it" or "doing it that way." No more worries about what is customary or what others in your industry might think. The gray is where your voice is lost. It is your crowd, your clutter, and your competition.

To stand out, you have to get out of the gray. You have to step left or right of the masses—step out of the mediocre middle where everyone else lives and works. When others are less, you must be more. When others are more, you must be less. Or just something totally different. You must be "always something," or "never something." You must be "so something," "too something," or "not at all something." But always, always, you must be too wonderful to miss.

To step out of the gray, you must push the envelope, stretch the page, and make yourself distinctive among the rest. Can you take it too far? Possibly. Just listen to your targets; they'll tell you. If you're operating in the gray zone now, there's probably little risk of going too far. How much do you really have to stretch to stand out? Sometimes you have to stretch a mile, sometimes just a step. It all depends on your particular gray.

Consider Your Context

To get out of the gray, you first have to find your gray, and that depends wholly on context. Wherever you want to get noticed, get attention, and achieve a specific result is your context. In fact, you have many contexts such as the industry and marketplace you compete in, as well as every place you put your marketing message.

Many people assume that, to stand out, you need to make things bigger, bolder, louder, stronger, faster, or shinier. Sometimes that's true. Sometimes it's the opposite. If everyone is trying to make things bigger, bolder, louder, stronger, faster, or shinier then you have only found another gray mass. Anytime "everyone" is involved, there is gray.

Therefore, before jumping into any marketing project or material, you must consider the context first to discern your gray and know what you need to step out of. You need to know what your message will be competing with for attention. If everyone is bold and loud, maybe you need to be light and subdued. If everyone is conservative, maybe you need to be playful.

Too often marketers launch into an advertising campaign or create a Website or brochure guided simply by what they think they should do or what they like. But that's not how your target sees it. Your target is looking at you and others like you. Your target is asking, "What's special or different about this one?" If it's not blatantly obvious, and really good, then you're stuck in that big gray ball of nothing special.

Marketers spend too much time scratching their heads trying to figure out what they should do when their best bet is to simply observe what they shouldn't do. When it's time to get a marketing message out there, look around and simply ask, *What is everyone else doing?* That's your first clue of what you absolutely must *not* do—not if you want to stand out. Context trumps all. It always matters, and it's always your best gauge as to what direction you need to take your message.

Most people simply don't take the time, or have the mindset, to diligently assess their context and their gray before going down a path that may or may not serve them. You can't stand out from the rest until you understand the rest.

Let's look at a couple examples of how this can work for you. Say I go to a standard business networking meeting donning my lovely Mickey Mouse hat—you know, the ears. I would definitely get noticed and maybe even get some attention. But, if I had no good story to tell, everyone would start elbowing their neighbors asking, "Who let the crazy lady in?"

If, instead, I walk in strutting that same hat while introducing myself as a travel agent and passing out promotions for a Disney vacation, I would be immediately promoted from crazy lady to brilliant marketer. I would stand out. I would get noticed, get attention, and likely sell some vacation packages. It definitely would help targets remember me.

I can speak firsthand because I've worn those ears to make this very point in speeches and seminars. Doing so made me memorable and helped me to generate more opportunities to speak. There is indeed reward in standing out in a good way.

Here's another terrific story of how considering context made stepping out of the gray exceptionally easy and effective.

I once helped a cattle rancher stand out with just this approach. He recruited my marketing expertise to help him sell his cattle through a popular magazine devoted to his specific breed. The advantage was that the readership was obviously interested in his type of cattle. The disadvantage was that every other advertiser was offering the same product. To be successful, we would really have to stand out. We would have to somehow connect with buyers to earn their favor amid many comparable competitors. It's not that odd of a situation. We all find ourselves competing in much the same arena all the time.

In this case, we knew we needed to be clever, so we started thinking like a marketer. Instead of plowing into production with some random advertisement that "followed form" and said what every other ad said, we assessed our context. It didn't take a lot of effort to detect the trend. Fellow advertisers displayed a picture of their bull or heifer and talked about their quality cattle. Some would try to be different by putting their grandchildren or puppy dog in the picture, or they would photograph their cattle in a field of Texas blue-bonnets. Making my customer stand out wasn't going to be much of a challenge after all. Not after we got smart about our context.

We took a 180-degree approach. We developed a series of half-page, black and white ads. We created cartoon sketches of cows in all sorts of humorous situations. The first ad featured the cow staring directly at the reader saying, "Let me tell you about my breeder." It got our rancher noticed.

It was a fresh idea, nothing like anyone else was doing, and completely outside the gray. We ran ads with cows lounging, wearing sunshades, and always being smart or funny. People would tell our customer how they couldn't wait to get the next issue to see what the cow would be doing next.

Assessing the context gave us clear direction about where we needed not to go, so it was much easier to develop a strategy that would make our rancher stand out. In this case, we were able to spend far less money and get a great deal more attention. And, yes, our rancher sold lots of cows.

So, how can you stand out in your marketplace? What is your competitive context telling you?

It Doesn't Take Much

The good news is that it doesn't take much to stand out. Individually, we can stand out by always being positive or dependable or any other adjective. We all know those who share a joke or interesting story every time we see them, so we label them as funny or interesting people. You too can stand out with something as simple as the way you dress, what you generally talk about, and how you interact with others. It doesn't take anything earth-shattering or mind-blowing. With these examples, it just takes repetition.

It is just as easy to make your business stand out. With service so bleak most everywhere, it's easy to be distinct if you just perform as every business should anyway. A little courtesy might be all you need to get noticed and get attention.

In my house, we have retained a particular painter for years because he is always incredibly polite, does a perfect job, cleans up well afterward, and overall makes the project really easy for me. It's always a wonderful experience to work with him and his team. All of those reasons are good reasons to continue to choose him. He gives us a good story to tell about him, but there's nothing extreme or crazy about it. He doesn't write us thank you notes or leave gift baskets. He doesn't have a wildly painted van or host big promotions. He just does a great job and is extremely professional and cordial doing it. But, because most painters don't come with all those attributes, at least not in my experience, he really shines through.

■

So where are you standing? Are you getting noticed and getting attention? Are you standing out in the way you want and need to achieve your desired results? Consider your context and step out of the gray.

Chapter 10

The Four Secrets to Standing Out
Drum roll please

I have come to observe that there are essentially four strategies for standing out. Like most marketing tenets, they are somewhat intertwined. While you're accomplishing one, you gain the compounding effect and benefit of another. Use each and all of these methods to help you stand out as an individual and as a company.

1. Do different things.
2. Do things differently.
3. Stir emotions; spread happiness.
4. Be consistent.

Let's take a closer look.

Do Different Things

Standing out is all about being different. After reading this chapter, you'll be quick to notice how often people say, "It stands out because it's different." It is easy to stand out when you do something no one else is doing, or at least no one else in your industry, market segment, or geography.

When Starbucks revealed their "new way" of serving up the coffee experience, the world raced to try their fresh idea. Cirque du Soleil has turned the model of "circus" on its head (and into many other odd positions). The Blue Man Group—well, what can I say? When you paint yourself blue, you're going to stand out. The good news is that you don't have to go to that extreme to be successful.

I once had a neighbor who grew a patch of Texas bluebonnets in his front yard. It was very odd really. Before long, he attracted an endless train of photographers and darling little toddlers in lacy dresses and overalls. Mothers couldn't wait to get their children's pictures taken in the sea of beautiful blue-bonnets. Needless to say, this man became very popular. He did something different and it got him noticed and got him attention. It was obvious he enjoyed the visitors, so he achieved his desired results.

One of my customers wanted to stand out with top CEOs, so we developed a program that included tailored marketing messages and fun toys like giant pencils and wind-up characters. It was a great departure from the standard mug and leather portfolio gifts, but it definitely got the customer noticed. It was different and it made targets smile, and they responded with new business. The cost and work were minimal, but the impact was huge.

To beat your competition, you can't be just a little better than they are. You have to do something different than they do. Anything goes as long as it is meaningful to the customer and helps you attract more of your ideal candidates.

Do Common Things Differently

This is the twist, mark, and signature you put on something common to make it uniquely your own. This is where you demonstrate your understanding that the "how" can be more important than the "what." When everyone is doing things the common way, you do them in a new and different way.

There is a lovely hotel in Dallas, Texas, that is well reputed for its five-star style and sophistication. I got lucky once in making a last-minute reservation for what I thought would be just another standard hotel stay. Instead it became an impressionable memory and one of my all-time favorite marketing stories.

The hotel has everything you would expect for its caliber—lavish decor, attentive service, and a host of amenities. Indeed I was made to feel special the second I stepped onto their property. On the way to my room, my bellman handed me a slick, four-color flyer on the history of the hotel. I didn't read it, but I was impressed to get it. I was staying in a hotel with history!

After reaching my room, he gave me a quick briefing on the shoe shining bag, the digital radio, fresh flowers in the bathroom, and other nuances that had me saying "wow" repeatedly. Now, let's not misunderstand. I have had the grateful opportunity to stay in several top-tier hotels before, but this one was different. About 30 seconds after my bellman wished me a good evening, there was a knock at the door. Being there alone, I was a little alarmed. I slowly opened the door to reveal a white-coated man carrying a large serving tray above his head.

"I'm sorry. You've got the wrong room," I told him. "No, Ma'am, compliments of the house," he said. Was he serious? Yes, fortunately he was. It was a welcome gift, all for me.

The man swept in with his beautiful tray that carried a carafe of tea, a silver covered dish, and a handwritten note. I thanked him excitedly and then quickly reached to reveal the present under the silver dome—a small blueberry bundt cake. I could hear the ting of the silver as the dome hit the plate as if to say, "Taddaaaa!" The note was sweet and succinct, simply thanking me for staying and encouraging me to tell them if anything could make my visit more comfortable—nothing groundbreaking, just kind and unexpected.

Their gift was a simple, inexpensive, and easy-to-execute gesture on their part, but it made a tremendous impact on me. Of course there's no other hotel in Dallas I'll ever stay at if I can help it, and you had better believe I'll be anxiously awaiting my bundt cake and iced tea. I will also continue to tell thousands of people about their hotel. Although I cannot point directly to it, I know I must be responsible for driving a decent amount of business their way. They deserve it for being such great marketers.

Another great example of standing out by doing common things differently is the little donut shop in my neighborhood that blessed us with a drive-through. That was reason enough for my family to punt our allegiance to the other guys who made us park and walk in. But the real genius from this small business is the rough-cut sign they posted next to the window with a listing and photo of their many selections. They even have a not-so-perfect color photo of their beverage selections. It's a little thing, but no other donut shop in town does it, and it makes a world of difference in the efficiency and ease of our morning rush. All it took was a little foresight to consider their customer's perspective.

We all know many businesses that do common things in uncommon ways, who understand that it's not just what they do, but how they do it that counts. It's the mulch shop that posts daily promotions for dirt using playful rock-and-roll lyrics; the gas station with really funny billboards and super clean restrooms; the oil change shop that has beautiful landscaping and that vacuums your car before they hand it back to you; the hotel with fun, themed rooms; and computer technicians who drive around in brightly painted, highly identifiable vehicles.

When people talk about companies that stand out because they do common things differently, they use expressions such as:

"There, they give you..."

"There, you get to..."

"What they do there is..."

Could your customers use these expressions to tell others about your company? How would they finish each sentence? If you're not sure, let that be your directive to step out of the gray and do something different than the rest.

Spread Happiness; Stir Emotions

The power of emotion cannot be underscored enough. Emotion is energy in motion, and when you stir intense feelings of happiness, you will definitely stand out. In fact, targets will beat a path to your door.

Making people laugh is a sure-fire way to stir happiness and get people talking about you. Company after company has earned millions of dollars by adding humor to their advertising. Aflac is a pure example of taking a dry topic and cranking it up with laughter. They have made themselves highly memorable and very successful with a mischievous duck. Personally, I'll stop cooking dinner just to catch his latest prank.

My customer who dared to send toys to top CEOs made them laugh and gave them a break from the madness of their day. He showed his targets that he was a different kind of company and hinted that working together would be fun.

You can spread happiness by applying one of the love languages described earlier. At Sonnier Marketing, we spread happiness every time we mail an invoice. We simply asked the question, *How can we make a great impression here?* Our answer landed with a way to stir positive emotions during a generally not-so-exciting moment in business. Now, with each invoice we send, we include a sealed motivational card, a wonderful little find that costs us all of $10 for a pack of 50 cards. Every time an accounts payable person receives our invoice, she also gets a smile. It's a wonderful thing when people tell you that they love getting your invoices! And, you can bet that we rarely have trouble getting paid. It's a simple thing for us, but it's a big impact for the person who is opening up bill after bill every day. In that context, we definitely get noticed and get attention. And, for regular customers, they know right away when they see our envelope that there's something inside just for them. Our inexpensive motivation cards spread happiness. They make us different. They make us stand out.

But the benefit goes even deeper. When you stir positive emotions, be they joy or inspiration or peace of mind, you send a message that there's more where that came from. Targets will think that if you are considerate here, you'll be considerate elsewhere and, until you prove them wrong, they will attach that perception to you.

Spreading happiness and stirring positive emotions will always make great things happen for your business.

Be Consistent

Consistency is glue. The other three methods will have lasting impact only if they are consistent. When you're always something or never something, you become that something. Being happy one day and a grump the next only makes you "normal" and in the gray. But always being upbeat and cheerful makes you a bona fide happy person. The same goes with your company. Giving terrific service one day and average service the next keeps you in the gray. But, always deliver a special experience by being consistent, spreading happiness, and maybe even doing common things in a different way, and you have stand out success.

Think about how we all talk about other companies. We will often start our stories with "they always" or "they never." They always give you a cookie when you leave. They never nitpick you or charge extra for that. They always run funny ads. They always say hello and make eye contact with you when you walk into the store.

Whatever it is, however seemingly insignificant, if it always happens or never happens, you have created something sticky. You have developed an identity that people can count on and will talk about.

Putting Them All Together

The cattle rancher's advertising campaign is a fine example of how several of these methods can interplay. He did a common thing in a different way by analyzing his context and going with the black and white ad approach instead of the expected four-color ad. He stirred emotions and spread happiness by bringing in comedy to a topic that usually takes on a standard set of dry talking points. And, he was consistent, running his campaign for many months so the series could become impressionable. Readers became accustomed to seeing the ads and would even comment that they couldn't wait to get the publication to see what the cow did next. It was pure marketing in action. It was conscious and deliberate. He considered his context, determined the gray, and stood out of it. He achieved his desired results of getting people to notice his ads, pay attention to them, and then call to buy his cattle. That is marketing at its best.

There is one word of caution I will leave you with, however. The more interesting and accepted your standout idea, the quicker you will attract imitators. In time, what you do and how you do it could become not so different. Through duplication, the marketplace could actually create a new gray. Pioneers typically enjoy only short windows of prominence and singularity. You will need to keep tight watch on your context to keep yourself out of the gray, however it evolves.

So go ahead. Do something different. Do common things differently. Spread happiness. Do one of them or all of them, just be consistent. You're sure to stand out.

Something More to Think About

▶ If your company went out of business today, would you be missed? Who would miss you? Who would never notice?

▶ How can you stand out in how you service your customers? What is the context you're competing in?

▶ How can you stand out in how you market your company externally? What is the context you're competing in?

▶ Do you stand out as a great place to work? Are you attracting ideal employees?

▶ Do your marketing tools and communications tell a unique story or could your competitor's name be easily substituted?

Tips 26–35
to Help You Put Marketing Into Action

26. **Give yourself a 30-day perception challenge.** With your List of Attributes complete, identify one item on which you intend to focus in the next 30 days. If, for example, you want to be perceived as creative, then commit to producing some "idea sheets" for your marketing tool chest. If, personally, you want to be perceived as a hard worker, commit to arriving to work an extra half hour earlier every day. Any small step can make big progress if you just start.

27. **Stand for something greater than yourself.** Be a company of consciousness. Promote more than just a product or service. Promote what your product or service stands for such as beauty, health, fiscal fitness, and environmental responsibility.

28. **Stand by your positioning statement.** A positioning statement can be extremely effective if it really means something. It must be more than just a few words attached to your logo. It must be a mantra by which you operate and it must be a central theme in all that you do, and certainly all of your marketing. If not, it's just meaningless fluff.

29. **Search a publication for your industry to identify the gray,** as well as who stands out and why. When something catches your attention, take a moment to discern why and then apply that learning in your own efforts to stand out. Even keep a file to refer back to when you need some creative assistance.

30. **Use colored envelopes.** Wouldn't you be more intrigued about a letter or package that arrived in a red, blue, or purple envelope? This is one of the easiest ways to stand out in the mail stack, to make your materials pop, and to further enforce your company's identity. Stand out with color.

31. **Send odd shapes and sizes.** Shake up the normal mail options with square envelopes, small note cards, and oversized postcards. Because they're different, they always stand out. Best of all is the bulky envelope. When people see and feel it, they have to know what's in there. Something as simple as a paper clip or rubber band can dramatically increase the success of your campaign. Just be sure it makes sense by tying it to your message. On all accounts, check with the postal service before committing. Sometimes rates can be considerably higher, and you'll definitely want to know that beforehand.

32. **Take some lessons from the hospitality industry.** No matter what kind of business you are, there's something worthwhile to be learned from an industry whose sole purpose is making customers feel good. Consider what makes a big impression on you when you're traveling and staying at hotels, as well as what frustrates you. How can you apply those observations to give your customers 5-star treatment?

33. **When on vacation, grab extra souvenirs for key customers,** vendors, associates, and anybody else you want to love you. They don't have to be big or pricey to make a big impact. All you need is a little something with

a note that says, "Please enjoy this small trinket from Bermuda. I saw it on vacation and thought of you." Wouldn't you be stunned and impressed to receive that package? It's truly the thought that counts here.

34. **Stand out with food.** There is little else that bonds people like food. Use it as one of your greatest marketing tools. Send food to break into hard-to-reach contacts. Send it to new customers, inactive customers, bestselling customers, everyone. Make a memorable splash with customized cakes and cookies. Send enough for the entire company or department so everyone knows you and loves you.

35. **Be equipped to please.** Have umbrellas, tissues, drinks, and other special touches handy for customers. The hair salon that allows a newly "cut and styled" customer to venture into the rain without supplying an umbrella has missed a big marketing opportunity (and made a customer very angry). Think of the small details that could make the difference between happy customers and ecstatic ones. You're sure to stand out, and people will not forget your kindness or your attention to detail.

Establish the Systems That Make Marketing Happen

Building your marketing machine.

Chapter 11

Making Marketing Practical, Focused, and Routine

Re-thinking how you make marketing happen

I'm guessing that you're pretty busy. I'm guessing that you have many great marketing ideas that never surface on your "urgent" list—at least not until your company starts to feel financial pressure.

If you have ever stressed over marketing, or if your marketing has ever suffered due to lack of money, time, and people power, then you are about to be liberated. I would never be audacious or short-sighted enough to proclaim that marketing doesn't need money, time, and people, but I can tell you with complete conviction that it can be done, and be successful, with a lot less than you think. It comes down to two things: thinking like a marketer and integrating marketing into everything you do every day.

When you think like a marketer, you look at things differently. When others see the details of the day as obstacles to marketing, you see them as a canvas for great marketing. In truth, the tedium of business comes with great power and opportunity to stand out and push your marketing forward. The details are assets. As a marketer, you know you must capitalize on every one of them.

But how do you manage them all? And how do you construct an external marketing effort that really does help you stir awareness, emotions, mindfulness, conviction, and word-of-mouth? How do you keep marketing constant and consistent? One of the greatest struggles for small and mid-sized businesses isn't just making marketing effective, but making it happen.

The answer is a system. With a solid, practical system in place, you not only make your marketing successful, you make it happen—almost in spite of yourself and under any circumstance. Even when you're chasing fires. With a good system, your marketing becomes focused, doable, and routine. It becomes streamlined and practically automatic. Before long, it becomes as natural and as common as making payroll, paying taxes, answering the telephone, and taking out the trash. No one challenges the fact that these duties have to happen. But what about marketing? There are no official rules and guidelines, no governing body. No one will yell at you or put you in jail if you don't actively market your business. But you will suffer. Even if you are successful, you won't achieve what you could have had you been aggressive and persistent in your marketing.

The right system—my system—will masterfully guide every step. You'll know exactly what to do and when to do it. You'll keep all of your pots stirred. And, you'll build and maintain marketing momentum for ongoing results. All of that frustration and overwhelment you feel about what to do and what to do next will have somewhere to go—a channel that can help you get the clarity you need to become unstuck and keep your marketing in motion.

There is nothing to hold you back any more. With your new mindset, an ocean of new marketing knowledge, and the system you're about to learn, you are ready to get clear, focused, and confident in your marketing. You're about to be the slickest, smoothest, raciest marketing machine! Hold on!

Getting a Good Plan

Many marketing directors and business owners spend exorbitant hours working up their official Marketing Plan. My experience is that most marketing plans are hollow, actionless documents that boast big ideas without giving anybody any direction about how to make them happen. As I tell my daughters, they need "less talk and more do."

Everybody wants to increase sales, retain customers, and overall grow business. There's nothing new there. But ask any marketing plan developer how she proposes to achieve those goals and she'll likely give you another general, predictable answer such as "get more customers" and "grow current customers." So again, I have to ask, "And how exactly do you intend to do that?" Eventually she gets frustrated, but she accepts that her plan is too vague, resembling more of a wish list for Santa than a working business strategy.

As always, we are called to drill down to the specifics for only there can we find the direction we need to make marketing happen and to make it work. The smaller your enterprise, the less margin for error. You must take the appropriate time and initial steps to develop a detailed blueprint of exact actions and timetables. Anything less will leave you exasperated, and your plan will be doomed to sit and die on the shelf as most marketing plans do.

Your plan does not have to be perfect, but it does have to exist. You don't need an impressive document like the kind you might present to a bank or venture capitalist, but you do need a written communication to clarify, direct, share, track, measure, and adjust your marketing activities. It should not be a long dissertation about who you are, what you could do, and what you should do. A real marketing plan is a design for action, one that lays out in no uncertain terms what, who, where, when, and how much. It is easy to follow, tells you what to do next, and integrates marketing into the day-to-day operation of your business so you can reach your business goals.

What Makes a Good Marketing Plan

A useful marketing plan is:

▶ **Written**—Committing your plan to paper is your first step to committing it to action. You need something tangible to work from, something you can share with others, check off as completed, and refer to as a daily guide of what you need to be doing that day to stir the pot in your business. Post it or make it available to everyone in your company. Marketing is always a team effort.

▶ **Specific**—A plan that lives in the clouds is just a book report and a futile exercise. A real marketing plan tells you exactly what to do and when to do it. Getting this level of detail down on paper may take a little time and effort, but it is your secret playbook. It makes all the difference in doing marketing and talking about it, and no marketing machine can run well without it.

▶ **Comprehensive**—Most plans, like most companies, focus only on external initiatives. By now you well know that this is only half your task. Your marketing plan must cover all aspects of your marketing inside and outside your business so they can be cohesively orchestrated. No doubt all activities become easier, and the results more profound, when they are.

▶ **Actionable**—The real measure here is whether you and your team know exactly what to do day-to-day to put and keep your marketing in motion. A good plan addresses not only the desired outcomes, but also the exact strategies and action steps that make those outcomes happen.

► **Fluid**—As events occur in and around your business, be it new trends, changes in the economy, or shake-ups in your industry, you must be ready to adapt and adjust, and so must your marketing plan. It must be a dynamic, living, breathing tool based on the reality of the day. It must always be circulating.

Turning Your Plan Into a System

Because marketing is inherent in everything you do, it requires paying attention to everything you do inside and outside your business. You have several pots on your stove at all times and lots of different ingredients in each one. There are some common elements, but no doubt there is a lot to be watched and to be stirred. Marketing is in the details and those details accumulate to shape your business and keep your targets mindful and moving in your direction. The only way to ensure that you manage and capitalize on these details as they come flying at you at high speeds and from every direction is to outsmart them with a system. A system is both your safety net and your magic formula for making marketing happen in spite of yourself. With a good system, you can:

► Make marketing automatic.

► Operate with clarity and confidence.

► Share the work so marketing gets done.

► Take advantage of the bounty of marketing opportunities inherent in your business every day.

► Stop reinventing the wheel every time.

► Keep your marketing goals in focus.

► Know marketing is happening even when you're doing other things.

► Take charge of your success.

Some people get clever and turn SYSTEM into a handy acronym for "Saves You Some Time, Energy, and Money." In terms of marketing, we may need to adjust that to "Saves Your *Sanity*, Time, Energy, and Money."

However you look at it, a system is an ordinary way to achieve extraordinary results, and every marketer needs that. Your customers need it, too. Customers want to work with people and companies who have their act together. They want to be able to depend on the products and services you offer, as well as the experience of getting them. That, as we have thoroughly discussed, is achieved through repetition, consistency, and constancy. Those, in turn, are accomplished through a system like the one you're about to learn.

Getting Organized

Before we get to the actual planning, the actual cooking, we have to get all of our ingredients together. Personally, I'm not the most organized of cooks. I enjoy creating on the fly, at least at the beginning of the project. But in the middle, when my pot starts to burn because I'm busy cutting vegetables, I remind myself that cooking could be easier, stress-free, and burn-free if I would just take the time to gather and prepare all of my ingredients before I started cooking. There's no skipping a step. Everything has to be done at one point or another. If I don't allow myself to get lazy, and force myself to get everything in order first, the experience of cooking—and its outcome—are significantly better.

So goes with your marketing. When you get anxious and don't gather your ingredients first, there can be trouble, sometimes at great expense. Likewise, when you get stuck because you haven't taken the time to get clear on the what's and the how's of your marketing, it's easy to push marketing aside. It's easy for marketing to get drowned out by the rush and roar of the urgent and the mundane. On all fronts, you must forcefully intervene. Marketing requires planning and preparation to be effective. Jumping in without forethought is careless and can be costly. Worse, without planning, you may never make deliberate marketing happen at all.

You must take the time to pre-think your marketing and prepare your ingredients. After that, it will hum and get easier as you go. Do first things first and let momentum take it from there to keep your business in a healthy state of circulation.

As Richard Koch says in his insightful book, *Living the 80/20 Way,* "Anything we do is much more difficult the first time and it gets progressively easier the more we do it, to the point where it becomes easier to do it than not do it." He also notes, "There is always a route that provides an elegant and relatively easy solution, a way to get much more of what we want for much less energy, time, money, and bother. All we have to do is find it."

You just did. Time to roll up your sleeves.

Chapter 12

Marketing Opportunities Here, There, and Everywhere

Putting what you have to work for you

As we have firmly established, everything is marketing and everything presents an opportunity for you to make a great impression and motivate your targets to decide that you are their best choice for the products and services you provide. When you think like a marketer, you harness these opportunities to stand out of the crowd, the clutter, and the competition. And, you turn your company into a marketing machine.

It is a waste of your time, money, and sanity to focus solely on the outside without making good due of what sits right under your nose and stares you in the face. You undermine everything you do outside by not focusing on everything you do inside.

You need both. And you need them well aligned and coordinated. First step: a tour of your business.

Uncovering Your Internal Marketing Opportunities

When we break down any business—your business—we find many moments when impressions are made. These are "moments of truth" when you get to show the world that you really are all that you purport yourself to be. They are identity in action.

In each moment, you can stand out with great impressions or you can follow the crowd with indifferent impressions. Shame on you if you make bad impressions. These moments are perfect opportunities to tell your targets what's in it for them and what you've done for them lately. You can also use them to sell, cross-sell, up-sell, and re-sell.

There is indeed good work to be done in every interaction, exchange, and communication, in every tool and piece of paper, in everything that is you and that represents you. As a marketer, you are on a quest to uncover every blank slate where you can add your logo, contact information, and marketing message. Everything is clay to be molded your way. Everything is part of the roux that can make your great business gumbo. Everything can serve you if you take the time and attention to put it to work for you. The best part is that many require only little effort and little money to make a big impact.

So let's peek and poke about your business. Get out your magnifying glass. We're looking behind the curtains and under the carpets. Opportunity is waiting!

What Is the Marketing Opportunity Here?

Marketing opportunities abound in your business. All you have to do is think like a marketer to find them and, of course, ask the questions, *What is the marketing opportunity here?* and *How can we make a great impression here?*

I have listed below many of the marketing opportunities inherent in almost every business. In no way is the list exhaustive, but it's a great start to help you uncover some tools and areas you may be neglecting.

You may be surprised at what you find, but I assure you that each and every item has marketing potential. (Everything is marketing, right?)

> *Internal opportunities that sound odd to you might be the very ones that could help you stand out.*

As you go through the list, note which ones apply to your business and, of those, which need improvement to make a great impression.

On major word of caution: Do not be quick to decide that an item does not apply to you. If you are an Internet business, "reception" may not resonate in the physical sense, but you still have a home page that has to usher in visitors and make them want to stay and click around.

Keep your mind open. Expand your thinking about what could work for you. If an item exists in your business in any way, it is a marketing opportunity on which to capitalize. Items that sound odd to you might be the very ones that could help you stand out.

As a marketer, you are charged and challenged to go where others do not go, so consider all possibilities. Everything counts and everything can help you. The tighter your budget, the more you need to stretch to find anything that could fuel your marketing engine. Your business holds a bounty of opportunities just waiting for you. Enjoy the fun of finding them.

Uncovering Your Marketing Opportunities

What marketing opportunities can you uncover and capitalize on in your business? Consider each item listed on pages 126–127 carefully. Check those that do apply or could apply to you. (Stretch your thinking.) Among those, note which need your attention to make great impressions.

It's All Marketing

Were you surprised by some of the things you saw there? Don't let the length of that list overwhelm you. Be excited that you have so many tools to help you build your business. If you were even capable of counting every opportunity, both stationery and fleeting, that you have every day in the normal operation of your business and interaction with prospects, customers, and other targets, the number could register in the hundreds or even thousands. Every communication, exchange, exposure, e-mail, and piece of communication counts. The best news is that you can capitalize on many for little or no money.

Take something as small and simple as your fax cover sheet, accounting statements, and invoices. They may seem purely administrative, but they are indeed marketing tools. I've already told you how my company turned the standard function of issuing invoices into a marketing moment with our motivational cards. Your fax cover sheet and every other administrative tool presents the same opportunity. These basic items come with a captive audience. You know people are looking at them, so why not rework them to include a list of your products and services or an announcement about your business? I have personally generated business from this little, no-cost idea. Each of your administrative tools is a marketing opportunity just waiting to be tapped. Any place that has your name on it in any way is a chance to put marketing into action.

So how do you know what to do with them all? How do you turn them into great impressions? Of course, every item is different and every business is unique, but you can always rest on the principles you've learned. Consider the context and step out of the gray. Ask, *What is the marketing opportunity here?* and *How can we make a great impression here?* to arrive at a great idea and something new. And, consider everything from your customer's perspective.

Some things simply need to be tweaked to include your company logo and contact information or your list of offerings. Some will require intense brainstorming. As a general rule, you can begin by thinking about what would make a customer say wow. What would turn an average interaction or exchange into a "taddaaa moment" like my visit to the hotel? Or, simply pretend to be a customer and walk through the process of being served by your own company. Important details miraculously surface when we step into our customers' shoes.

Another tool to help you turn these everyday occurrences into big marketing moments is to pull out your newly devised List of Attributes. Assess how you could achieve your desired adjectives and attributes in each item or communication.

Finally, there is a particularly useful tool I developed to help me get clear when developing a marketing letter or other promotional piece. You'll learn more about it in Phase 5, but an aspect can help you here so I'll give you a heads-up. It's called the **Know-Think-Feel-Do formula** and it's a simple exercise of asking four questions before you venture into any marketing project or message. Use these questions here to help you arrive at a way to make the most of every marketing opportunity. With each item, just ask:

▸ In this situation, what is important for my target to **know** about us?

▸ For our target to **think** about us?

▸ For our target to **feel** about us?

▸ What do we want our target to **do** as a result of this interaction, exchange, communication, or tool?

Don't expect to be able to tackle everything on the list right away. Just choose a few items that would make a great impact and build from there. Like everything else in marketing, you'll find that once you apply your great ideas in some areas, you'll be able to repeat and repurpose your approach in others. The process gets easier as you go.

Marketing Opportunity	Applies to Me	Needs Attention
Business location	❑	❑
Building facade and parking lot	❑	❑
First impressions	❑	❑
Reception	❑	❑
Receptionist	❑	❑
Customer areas	❑	❑
Non-customer areas	❑	❑
Décor	❑	❑
Floorplan	❑	❑
Floors and ceilings	❑	❑
General inside appearance, maintenance	❑	❑
Employee break room	❑	❑
Service offering/performance	❑	❑
Proposals, estimates	❑	❑
Sales presentations	❑	❑
Invoices	❑	❑
Collection procedures	❑	❑
Warranties and guarantees	❑	❑
Terms and conditions	❑	❑
Policies and protocols	❑	❑
Customer service	❑	❑
Options and flexibility	❑	❑
Delivery	❑	❑
Price	❑	❑
Sales tickets	❑	❑
Statements	❑	❑
Fax cover sheet	❑	❑
Forms and contracts	❑	❑
Shipping tickets, receipts	❑	❑
Letterhead and business cards	❑	❑
Brochures	❑	❑
Menus and service offers	❑	❑
Website	❑	❑
Voice mails	❑	❑

Marketing Opportunity	Applies to Me	Needs Attention
On-hold messages	❑	❑
Telephone skills	❑	❑
E-mail signatures	❑	❑
Cleanliness/organization of goods	❑	❑
Point of sale	❑	❑
Sales team	❑	❑
Sales support	❑	❑
Service after the sale	❑	❑
Hours of operation	❑	❑
Restrooms	❑	❑
Appearance of team members	❑	❑
Uniforms	❑	❑
External signage	❑	❑
Internal signage	❑	❑
New customers	❑	❑
Holidays	❑	❑
Boxing and packaging	❑	❑
Customer questions	❑	❑
Timeliness	❑	❑
Lagniappe (something extra)	❑	❑
Sound	❑	❑
Lighting	❑	❑
Smell outside and inside	❑	❑
Selling at the counter	❑	❑
Bags, boxes, and packaging	❑	❑
Database building; collection of contacts	❑	❑
Furniture and effects	❑	❑
Helpful items for customers (umbrellas, pens)	❑	❑
Wall hangings	❑	❑
Computer system	❑	❑
Other marketing opportunities in your business:		
_____	❑	❑
_____	❑	❑
_____	❑	❑

Chapter 13

Identify Your Common "Service Points"

Making the most of important situations

Now that you have identified individual marketing elements, let's identify specific marketing moments. I call these *service points*. They are those standard situations, occurrences, exchanges, events, and interactions with targets of every type—customers, prospects, associates, vendors, staff members, anybody—that occur during the normal function of business.

Service points carry tremendous marketing weight. The consequences of neglecting them, or fouling them up, are costly. They are the moments when you relate with customers in some important and meaningful way: when you earn a customer, when you lose a customer, when a customer becomes a large customer or an inactive one, when you have to tell a customer no or that you've made a terrible error, or when you get a new referral from an old customer.

Service points are those emotionally-charged moments when a great impression is of great necessity and a bad impression comes at great consequence. Service points always matter and they matter big. That means you absolutely must have a system to identify them and respond appropriately and strategically. In each moment there is opportunity and responsibility to ensure only the best of emotions.

Let's take a look at the glorious event of earning a new customer. This is unquestionably a terrific and opportune moment. You just hit success. You just reeled one in after all that time, money, and hard work to stir awareness, emotions, and mindfulness. It's time to celebrate! For some companies, earning a new customer means ringing the bell and starting the parade. For most everyone else, it means absolutely nothing but the verbal thank you they mutter to the customer while processing her credit card. Those companies are absolutely not marketing machines. Any company who does not recognize and relish in this big moment of business has a lot of junk in their gumbo and a lot of work to do. Let that never be you.

Earning a new customer is always one of your most significant marketing events, and there must be no error in following through every single time. For that, you need a system. You need a protocol to make sure every new customer is identified and celebrated appropriately.

There are many important service points in every business. Below are some of the most common. These critical junctures in your day-to-day operation must, by all means, be considered carefully and strategically. They must be handled and handled to the best of your marketing ability.

Take a careful look at the following list. Do the same exercise of noting which do and could apply to you and which need attention to be killer marketing moments. Begin immediately to develop processes and protocols for each applicable item. This is some of the most important marketing you will ever do internally, so make it a priority and keep it under careful watch. The success of all other marketing is dependent upon, or at least affected by, what you do in these important business situations.

Service Point	Applies to Me	Needs Attention
A prospect becomes a new customer	❏	❏
A customer becomes inactive	❏	❏
A customer reaches a high sales level	❏	❏
You receive a new inquiry of any kind (Web, call-in, referral)	❏	❏
You present an estimate, quotation, or proposal	❏	❏
You send an invoice or statement	❏	❏
You answer the telephone	❏	❏
You communicate to a customer any way for any reason	❏	❏
You have to tell a customer no	❏	❏
You transact a purchase	❏	❏
A customer becomes angry or has a complaint	❏	❏
You make an error	❏	❏
You win a contract	❏	❏
A customer renews a contract	❏	❏
A customer doesn't renew a contract	❏	❏
A customer wants to return a product or be reimbursed for service	❏	❏
It's a holiday or special selling season	❏	❏
A customer has something exciting or tragic happen in his life or business	❏	❏
Business rocks along as usual	❏	❏

Making the Most of Your Service Points

To appropriately address these service points, and use them to their fullest advantage, you must develop standard protocols for responding to each. This is what I call the **When-Then formula**. When X happens, the company responds with Y. For example:

When the company earns a new customer, the customer receives a particular note and a particular gift.

When a customer becomes inactive, the company responds with four specific steps. And they are...

This is the beginning of your system. It is the program by which your company identifies and appropriately responds to common situations every single time. There is no guesswork. There is no wondering. You establish the what and the when. You decide the who and the how. Then you step and repeat, step and repeat. Every time X happens, you respond with Y. You create and develop the processes and protocols and then integrate them into all of the other standard actions of your business. Before long, these processes become a natural part of doing business, just like taking out the trash when the bin is full or putting on your happy voice when the phone rings. There is no difference.

The When-Then formula is essential to standardizing your marketing so you don't have to recreate your steps every time, or worse, worry that important service points are overlooked. If you do nothing else but put this formula to work for a handful of critical service points in your business, you will make a dramatic impact on your marketing.

Service points are the moments when your image and identity are tested most, and when they must converge with perfect precision. There is great risk and great potential. You can stir the right emotions or the wrong ones. You can lead a customer to conviction or you can turn them away. The key is having a pre-thought system to ensure diligent action and correct action, just like Chick-fil-A and my neighborhood postal service. By the way, the Know-Think-Feel-Do formula works beautifully with service points, too.

■

I hope it is increasingly clear how the core doctrines of marketing interplay and inter-relate in everything you do. Everything is circular and intertwined. Nothing you do stands alone or works in isolation. Good done in one area helps to advance another. Everything you do either moves your marketing forward or backward.

What's Your Y?

Your next step in developing your company's marketing system is to clearly identify the service points that happen in your business and to determine a response plan for each. For the first pass, do not limit yourself in any way. Write down whatever comes to mind no matter how outlandish it may sound. Capture your ideas as they come with no respect to time, money, people, or practicality. You can scale back your plans later, but for now, live in an ideal world. Just note what you consider to be the ideal approach and keep moving.

Let's look at an example of how a business-to-business service provider might respond in the common situations of earning a customer and losing a customer.

Service Point	Desired Response
Earn a new customer.	▪ Send personalized note from company president along with cake for entire customer company or department. ▪ Send "New Customer Welcome Packet" with bio sheets of key players and service staff, company phone numbers, tip sheets, and promotional item. ▪ Transfer customer from prospects database to customer database. ▪ Announce new customers at weekly staff meeting.
Customer officially becomes inactive or lost.	▪ Define "inactive." ▪ Establish reporting system to identify inactive customers monthly. ▪ Send "we miss you" card and incentive to customer. ▪ Have salesperson make personal contact to determine reason for inactivity or loss. ▪ Monitor customer status for 90 days. ▪ Review best steps at the end of 90 days.

From these short examples, we can develop a clear action plan. With the new customer, the company will need to establish a system to regularly identify new customers, such as a weekly report run by Accounts Receivable. In that case, the AR representative knows to run the report each week, and the marketing director knows to implement the New Customer Protocol each week. In addition, the new customer note and its packaging needs to be developed, but once that is done, it is ready to go every week. Same with the New Customer Welcome Package. This is a terrific tool to put a face on the company, make the customer feel special, and impart some important knowledge to make the customer's experience and relationship with the business more pleasant and productive. Once it is developed, it's just an off-the-shelf grab every time the company earns a new customer. Easy, easy. As the marketing director prepares these items, she knows to update the company database so it stays current.

With the inactive customer example, the company would need to establish the terms and conditions that officially make a customer inactive. Then, on whatever schedule makes sense, the marketing director would send the already-produced "We Miss You" card, and the salesperson would contact the customer and report progress in the next sales and marketing meeting. The company would then determine the best course of action during the next 90 days and follow through. The calendar would be noted at the end of those 90 days so the company could determine if other action was necessary, such as a more aggressive approach or re-categorizing the contact to a lower ranking in the company's prospect management system.

All of these specific action steps come from the simple process of working through the When-Then formula. From these two examples, we get a quick list of items to be produced, a few specific assignments for staff members (your marketing champions), and a few items to add to the company's official Marketing Calendar.

This is essentially all it takes to make a sound, actionable marketing plan. In just a few minutes of discussion, you can determine your When-Then scenarios and play out how they should ideally work to make the most of each service point. From there, you just make a few assignments (with deadlines of course), develop a few standard tools, and you're off and running. Marketing is put into motion with a little thought and a few easy steps.

Marketing, at least in these areas, becomes routine and automatic. The more you do it, the more natural it becomes in the fiber of your day-to-day. And, you will certainly see results from your efforts.

So what are the service points that happen regularly in your business? Use the worksheet on page 133 to guide you in developing your When-Then scenarios to take advantage of the critical service points in your business.

Service Point Planning Guide			
When	Then	Champion	Timing
Tools to Be Produced:			
Specific Processes to Be Established:			
Other Next Action Steps:			

Chapter 14

So Many Tools to Work With

Choosing what works for you

Internally and externally, you have a host of tools available to help you put every marketing idea into action. With each of these, you want to ask yourself, *How could I use this to help me make the right impressions?* Maybe you need more tools working for you. Maybe you need to scale back and focus on those that really produce. This is all part of the constant tweaking required to keep your marketing plan productive—and practical. Again we can take more good advice from Richard Koch in *Living the 80/20 Way*:

"Eighty percent of results come from 20 percent of activities. What are things that truly produce results in your work? Do more of them. Do them better. Forget everything else."

So now we look at another list, or rather the continuation of the internal activities that can make all the difference in your marketing impact and your external marketing effectiveness. These are more areas in which you must stir awareness, emotions, mindfulness, conviction, and word-of-mouth. The key difference in this list is that there is no deciding. Every single item is relevant and necessary for any business. Every single item must be managed from a marketing standpoint. Your tactics and execution may be different than other types of businesses, but everything applies.

Internal Marketing Tools for Every Business

► Proficiency of telephone skills

► Marketing training and mindset of the entire team

► Clear company vision

► Clear understanding of the company's role in the life of its customer

► Standard processes and tools for common service points

► Tracking of all inquiries

► Tracking of marketing success

► Qualifying prospects according to an Ideal Customer Profile

► Cross-promotion of services and departments

► Refined answer to "What do you do?"

► Up-selling at every opportunity

► Well-crafted answers to common customer questions

► Clear answers to 10 reasons to do business with you and your customer's question, "What's in it for me?"

► Well-managed and growing database

► Staff job descriptions incorporating marketing roles and functions

► Defined marketing goals of the company overall

► Defined marketing goals by department

► System to keep staff abreast of marketing activities

► Method to keep staff thinking, acting, and communicating like a marketer

External Marketing Tools

After all these lists, I would be remiss not to include one for your many external marketing tools. No doubt your options are plentiful and varied in the categories of ease, cost, and reach to your target. Use it to consider your choices when developing your specific external marketing strategies.

- Company brochure
- Company newsletter (print or electronic)
- Mass e-mail campaigns
- Coupons
- Birthday cards to customers
- Customer surveys
- Direct mail letter campaigns
- Over-sized, under-sized, and regular-sized postcards
- Open house and other company events
- Referral promotion program
- Advertising specialties
- Advertising in general
- Speaking events
- Participation in industry organizations
- Networking events
- Social networking

- Customer seminars, Webinars, and teleseminars
- Small-group presentations
- Public service
- Trade shows
- Website
- Podcasts
- Blogs
- Online videos
- Internet marketing
- Lunch meetings
- Public relations
- Sponsorships
- Testimonials
- Case studies
- Product samples
- DVDs and CDs
- Articles
- Tip sheets
- Buttons
- Uniforms and other wearable marketing
- Signage
- Flyers
- Doorhangers
- Brochures at neighboring businesses
- Asking for the order

Make an Actionable Marketing Plan

If you want to be successful without unnecessary hassle, then you absolutely must create an actionable marketing plan. It will save your sanity, time, money, and energy. It will give you the almighty direction you have always wanted in building your business. It will help you operate with clarity and confidence. It is an absolute must if you are to be a marketing machine. And, it's so much easier than you think.

You have already begun the thinking process by determining your service points and their action plans. You have already identified many tools to help you execute your plan. You are on your way. In truth, if you stopped right here, you would still be far ahead of most companies. But then you wouldn't totally be a marketing machine, and that's the goal. So let's explore the system that I have used repeatedly with customers and in my own business to make marketing practical, routine, and automatic.

It's called the SMAC Marketing Plan Detail™. SMAC is an acronym of my company, Sonnier Marketing & Communications, Inc. I love the way it sounds and I love telling people I'm going to SMAC them on the head with my spoon to get them thinking like a marketer. But it's not all fun and games. SMAC also stands for Smart Marketing Applied Consistently, and that's what successful marketing is all about. It's also what this system is about—to help you be a smart marketer every day in everything you do internally and externally.

I have used the SMAC system very successfully for a wide variety of businesses. Some companies were devout in their development and implementation. Others used the program to boost impact in a few weak areas. I certainly encourage you to take it all the way, to make it a comprehensive plan for your business. But, it's perfectly scalable if you must take it in parts.

SMAC Marketing Detail

Take a moment to study the Detail form on page 153. This outlines the components you must consider in developing your actionable marketing plan. The form is a valuable guide for discussion and planning, though you will likely want to create a digital spreadsheet to help you extract and organize its parts. Even when you aren't doing sophisticated planning, the Detail is a terrific tool to help you think through any marketing endeavor large or small. The same considerations apply whether you're making big plans or executing a single project.

The Parts

As always, a plan begins with a goal. For each goal, you will need to drill through several layers of details including:

▶ The **target audience** of that goal

▶ The **strategies** that could help you achieve that goal

▶ The **specific action steps** required to make each strategy happen

▶ The **champion or person responsible** for each action step

▶ The **deadline or timetable** by which each action is to be completed or the strategy enacted (for example, weekly, monthly, quarterly, and so on)

▶ The **budget** if any money is required

▶ The **metric or measurement** that will determine if your strategy is successful

Let's take them one by one.

Your Goals

I know you have goals. But before you jump into them, take a few steps back. Are you clear on the mission of your company? Are you clear on your role and contribution to your marketplace? Do you have a vision of what you want your business to be?

One of the most important and eye-opening things I ever did for myself and my business is to articulate these answers on paper. Suddenly I had direction like I never had before. Today, I carry a copy of my mission and vision statements in my daily organizer so I can be reminded of what I need to work toward every day. It keeps me grounded and focused on making the right choices about where I dedicate my time and energy. When someone asks me to do something outside of that realm, it's easy for me to say no.

Personally, I'm on a mission to be a difference-maker using the talents I've been given and the skills I have worked my entire career to hone. I want to help you realize how marketable you are. I want to help you do good things for your business because I know that will translate into good things for your life. I want to enlighten, inspire, and equip you with the mindset and tools you need to spread your message, so you can give more gifts to more people. So when I'm making my own Marketing Detail, I focus on the goals that will help me achieve my overall mission. There are many things I could do, and would like to do, but achieving my mission and vision supersede everything else.

Now it's your turn. What do you want to happen in your business today? What are your goals for this month? This year? Next three to five years? Next 10 years? You need to know so you can take calculated steps in that direction. Commit your goals to paper. If you have staff, do it as a team. If you don't have staff, call on a trusted advisor to help you. Goals are just wishes until they become formalized. Writing them down makes them real. As you look over your list of goals, make sure you keep your mission and vision in mind. You may need to edit some goals out to keep you on your path.

There are common goals in every business. Every company wants more sales, more customers, and more sales from current customers. Get specific. How much more in sales? How many more customers? One extra dollar and one extra customer satisfies a wish for "more," but that's likely not enough to make your business soar.

> *Goals are just wishes until they become formalized. Writing them down makes them real. As you look over your list of goals, make sure you keep your mission and vision in mind.*

Once you note the obvious goals, take some time to really think through all aspects of your business. Goals can be anything. There are no rules or limits here. One goal could be that your staff works better as a team. That's certainly a benefit to your business.

Hold your guard against the gremlins that like to creep in with discouragements like, "That could never happen" or "Don't get crazy." Anything can happen and "crazy" has made a lot of people crazy successful and crazy rich. After all, aren't you shooting for "crazy good"? Get all of your goals down as you wish them. Worry about reality later. You never know how far your new marketing system can pull you.

On a Technical Note

As you work up your goals list, be certain to identify true goals and not strategies. Those will come next. A goal is an aim, condition, or situation you want to exist. It is a result or outcome. As you declare your goals, write them to reflect what you want to be or have on a large scale. They are the "what's," not the "how's." For example, instead of saying that your goal is "to promote a marketing mindset throughout the company," say it is "to achieve and maintain a marketing mindset throughout the company." Instead of saying you want "to open a second location," say you want to "have two locations." The difference may seem subtle, but a slight change will help you keep a clear distinction between goals and strategies. Express your goals with concrete verbs such as *be, earn, generate,* and *have.*

Some goals to consider for your marketing plan are:

- Overall sales of the company
- Profitability
- Sales and/or profitability by service/product area, department, or other category
- Number of customers retained; volume of repeat business
- Number of new customers desired; volume of business from new customers
- Geographic reach
- Positioning in the marketplace
- Perception in the marketplace
- Customer ratings
- Mindshare
- Distribution avenues
- Type of customers attracted (ideal targets or any targets)
- Caliber of employees recruited
- Internal marketing mindset
- Capitalization of internal marketing opportunities
- Company image and identity
- Company personality and culture
- Progression toward long-term goals

Whatever your goals, be sure to add:

▶ Stir awareness

▶ Stir emotions

▶ Stir mindfulness

▶ Stir conviction

▶ Stir word-of-mouth

Make a copy of the Marketing Plan Detail for each of your goals and write one goal in the first column of each page. You're on your way!

Target Audience

For each goal, note its specific audience. These are your "pots" to be stirred. Some goals will target only one group; some will target several. For ease in completing your Detail, you may want to use these abbreviations:

PRO .... Prospect

CC .... Current Customer

IC .... Inactive Customer

EE .... Employees

MED .... Media

VEN .... Vendor

ASSOC .... Associate

Now step back to look at all of your worksheets. Do you have each of your target audiences represented somewhere? Are all of your pots accounted for? At this point, it's a good idea to think about your goals from the perspective of each target audience. What are the specific goals you have for new prospects, vendors, media, and all of your other important target groups? When you frame your thinking this way, you may add an extra goal or two to your plan. Marketing is never linear. It takes on many forms, pulls you in all directions, and wraps you around a few times before it lets you go. You may need to look at things from a few different perspectives before your plan can be considered complete. The more you work your plan, the more holes, connections, and possibilities you'll find. That just means your structure is taking shape. Don't stress or overpressure yourself to get it right, just reward yourself for getting it down. Remember that your plan is supposed to be fluid. You're going to be adding and adjusting things all the time. That is a natural part of the process and part of what makes marketing fun. There's always something new to do and discover.

The Process
Outline Strategies to Accomplish Each Goal With Each Target Audience

Now it's time to really get things cooking. It's time to think about all of the "how's." These are your strategies—thoughtfully constructed methods to help you achieve your objectives. Your strategies should start with action words and they are likely to be hefty ones like *identify, establish, collaborate, cross-promote, develop, implement,* and *conduct.* We talk in terms of strategies all the time when we make statements such as "we need to" and "we should." This is where you get to capture all of those good ideas.

Developing strategies is usually the most difficult stage of the program. Sometimes it's difficult to know what exactly will make a goal happen. After all, you probably think about it incessantly, and it's still confusing to you. Not only that, the success of the entire program hinges on what you put here, so it needs to be right. Or does it? Some strategies will be obvious to you. Some will be shots in the dark. Most marketers do more trial and error than they would care to admit. There's nothing wrong with that. When you think like a marketer and apply everything you've learned here, you will be able to make smart judgments about what will yield good returns. Sometimes you will be right; sometimes you will be surprised. But that's just how marketing goes. As long as you follow marketing principles and apply the smart lessons taught here, your risks will be minimized.

If you are at a total loss of what to do, hire a marketing professional to help you. Or, refer to your list of marketing tools to jumpstart ideas. Most importantly, don't over-think or over-analyze at this stage. Don't concern yourself with what is feasible or practical. Think only about what is possible. Think about what you would do if there were absolutely no restrictions of time, money, or human resources. You can revise and edit later, but if you don't capture the idea, you won't have the power of it. Sometimes just throwing ideas "out there" creates a magical chain of events that we could never consciously orchestrate. Voicing goals and plans is extremely powerful.

Let me digress with a little story to prove my point. One of my goals has always been to have a professional office for my business. I worked out of my home for many years, and though it never bothered me really, it became an issue when I started growing and needed to expand my company. I always wanted the office, but I would have never officially written it down as a goal because it just wasn't possible—so I thought.

Through a very odd and serendipitous chain of events, my husband and I were able to purchase a new property on a very desirable and highly valued street in Houston. We would have never imagined it, but in a snap, we were there. Impossible things happen all they time, and they can happen to you. Capture every goal and strategy that comes to mind no matter how outlandish it seems.

Break Strategies Into Action Steps

This is where the rubber meets the road and where most marketing plans never go. This is where you really start to get some direction as you determine the specific action steps that will bring your goals to fruition. Review the sample Detail on page 154 to see how your plan starts to take shape in this step.

Until now, you may have been recycling the material you've been hashing and rehashing in your brain or used in another marketing plan. Now it's time to go deeper and explore new territory. It's time to decide the small steps that will make big leaps in your marketing and your business.

For every single strategy, brainstorm the one, few, or many steps that will put that strategy into action. Be very detailed and specific as you create possibly numerous line items for each strategy.

A heavyweight goal such as increasing sales 15 percent will become a manageable to-do list of simple actions like *call, mail, research, assign, send, write, recruit,* and *choose.* Suddenly your big dreams will become quite doable. Your task list may be long, but everything on it will be manageable and easily executable by you or someone else. Later, as if by magic, you'll reach your goals and you'll wonder how it all happened. And I'll remind you—one stir at a time.

Assign a Champion to Each Action Step

If you are a solo entrepreneur, you will find your initials in all of these fields. But try not to. You may not be fully qualified for some things and require professional assistance. With others, you may be perfectly capable, but your time would be better spent elsewhere. Reach out for help to make success happen faster. Many talented high school and college interns would love to help you. Or, maybe you need to finally buy that software to increase your efficiency. In a world of virtual assistants and endless time-saving devices and programs, you have countless resources at your fingertips. The smaller your business, the more you'll need to leverage your time and energy. If you do have staff, share the duties. Everyone is a marketer, and everybody benefits when marketing succeeds (and suffers when it gets stymied or bogged down). Spread the duties to spread the wealth.

Assign a Deadline or Time Schedule to Each Action Step

To keep your marketing moving, you will need to assign a deadline or timetable to every action step where appropriate. Some items will require definite dates while some will dictate a schedule of regularity such as weekly, monthly, and quarterly events. As you initially develop your plan, just choose what feels comfortable at the moment. After you've completed your plan and start to create some of the suggested tools, it will become apparent if you were a bit over-zealous with your time schedule. It almost always happens. The timetable will show 150 items to be completed in 90 days and five to be done in six months. No big deal. You will need to work through each goal sheet before you can see how your dates fall and intersect. You can make them more realistic then.

Determine Costs or Establish Budgets for Each Item

If a strategy or action item requires money, make note of it in the budget column. If you aren't sure, make a guess and correct it later. Seeing everything in one place will certainly help you prioritize where and how money is spent, and help you establish your overall marketing budget.

Identify a Means to Measure Each Action Plan

Tracking results is a crucial step. Wherever possible, determine a metric to help you discern how a program is working. You need reliable data to know when you need to crank up your activities, tone them down, or tweak them in some way. Some data collection will be easy, such as sales and Website activity. Others will require an established process such as asking and recording how new prospects found you. Certainly the higher the number in the budget column, the more important it is that you track activity. In all cases, the more and tighter you track results, the greater your results will be.

Final Steps

When you have completed the SMAC Marketing Detail for all of your goals and their respective strategies, you will likely have many sheets of paper. If you haven't already put this data into a digital spreadsheet, you may want to do so now. It will be the most efficient way to organize, manage, and extract the information you will need for your next step—developing the tools that make your system work.

Getting Your Tools Together

Once you have worked through the fine details of each of your marketing goals and their specific strategies and action plans, you will need to reshape them into a form that you can work with day-to-day. Here are a few tools that will make executing your plan very easy:

Goals List

Stirring mindfulness begins at home. To keep you and everyone focused on the big picture every day as you make choices and decisions, post a list of your company goals and the respective audiences they target. Your team must remain clear on what the company is working toward.

To-Do Lists

This is where things start to get really interesting—and really effective. To move on all of those action steps, you'll need some to-do lists. If you have keyed your plan into a spreadsheet program, it will be extremely easy to organize and extract data. Output a list of action steps sorted by person responsible and by date. Now you can make any necessary adjustments on time and deadlines. With this list, everyone knows exactly what they need to do to make the big picture happen.

Task Summary Sheet

This is where you outline all activities that are to be done with some regularity, be it daily, weekly, monthly, quarterly, and so on. Maybe it's the weekly check for new customers who need to be celebrated, your monthly newsletter or ezine, that quarterly review for inactive customers, or the annual customer survey. Create a Task Summary sheet that lists actions for each timetable noting the activity and its assigned champion. (See example on page 155.) Post it alongside your Goals List on the company bulletin board or company Intranet. Update and discuss these items in regular manager and staff meetings.

Marketing Calendar

The final, and perhaps most important support tool, is your official Marketing Calendar. (See example on page 156.) This is your ultimate guide for keeping your marketing moving and on track. I highly suggest that you make it as visually simple and appealing as possible. Everyone involved must be able to see at a glance what's happening and what they are assigned to do.

You can create your Marketing Calendar manually or via spreadsheet, beginning with a list of all deadlines established in your Detail. Then add all routine events from your Task Summary sheet. Be very detailed and very thorough. Note everything that is time-relevant and time-driven. Think ahead and work backward on all events and projects that require planning such as trade shows and advertising campaigns. Note all related deadlines such as reserving space, submitting files, mailing announcements, and going to press.

Once you have created your Calendar, take a giant step back to view it from the perspective of each of your target groups. In fact, you may want to color code items by target audience to make this easy. When your plan becomes visual this way, it will make obvious any holes in strategy or hiccups in timing. You'll see how aggressive you're really being with each target group and if you need to make any adjustments in the flow of your messaging.

Your Marketing Calendar is invaluable. There is absolutely no better way to gain clarity and get a strong handle on where your marketing is and where it's going. It is your ultimate guide day-to-day to put and keep marketing in action. Keep it current and keep it posted.

Standard Communications

As you work through your Detail, the need for specific marketing communications and materials will surface. These should be developed right away. After that, you can forget about them, at least for a while. You want them ready to grab and go when the need arises. That's how marketing becomes automatic.

Master Marketing Book

You will thank me for this suggestion. Simply fill a large 3-ring binder with plastic sheet protectors to house all of your marketing samples. Every time you develop an ad, direct mail piece, letter, ezine, broadcast e-mail, anything, make a copy for "the book." Make a quick note of when the communication went out and generally to whom, as well as the name and location of its digital back-up. This will serve several terrific and useful purposes including to:

▶ Keep staff apprised of what's happening with your marketing and aware of what targets are receiving.

▶ Make it easy to extract and repurpose text and concepts, thereby shortcutting future projects.

▶ Surprise you with how much you've done.

▶ Help you identify inconsistencies in message and design as you see everything in context and in relation to one another.

▶ Give you a great scrapbook and sample of your progress.

Just Start

In all of my years in marketing, I have found no approach to marketing planning simpler than the program I just described to you. I know how easy this one can work. I know with absolute certainty that it can give you the direction you need to take action and put marketing into motion. I know it can help you make marketing automatic. You won't know this until you start putting pen to paper, until you work a goal all the way through the thinking process, and until you have all of those tools developed and organized to tell you what to do and what to do next. You just have to start. You have to give it a chance and you have to experience it for yourself. If you are serious about being a smart, aggressive marketer and giving your business the opportunity to reach its full potential, you need to just sit down and get to work. There is no other way. Stop reaching for something new to save you. This is as simple as it gets, barring hiring someone else to do all the work for you.

Marketing does not have to be complicated, difficult, expensive, or overly time-consuming. You have so much to work with right now. All you have to do is think like a marketer and take advantage of the bounty of tools and opportunities that exist right now, right under your nose. You just have to pick up your pen and start working through our Marketing Detail.

With the very first step, you start to stir things up. You activate ideas you never had. You see connections you never noticed. And suddenly, almost miraculously, things start to fall in place. All of the things that bewildered you about what to do externally will somehow dissolve as you start working through all of the possibilities of how. You'll see how one activity can build and play off another. You just have to start. You have to start stirring and then keep stirring.

I live this program every day. I know the wonders it can do if you will trust the process and keep the wheels in motion. There are no more excuses. There are no more reasons to put marketing on hold. Marketing couldn't be any easier than this, and now you know how to make it work step-by-step. It's time for less talk and more do.

If you install one good program to address an important service point, you will have done significant work for your business. If you develop one standard tool and regular program to help you get your marketing message out there, you will have made important progress. Remember that you cannot be everywhere all the time, and you don't need to be.

Even after you have worked through your plan, if it is not practical for you to do all that you've masterminded, don't stress about it. Pick one thing you know you can get done, or one thing you know will generate results, and build from there. Your SMAC Marketing Detail will pull you, and your instincts will guide you. Each step will be easier because of the last. Results will happen and they will compound. You have nothing to lose and so much to gain.

Something to Think About

▶ What marketing opportunities in your business can you uncover and put to work for you? What service points are most important to address right now?

▶ What marketing goals do you need to work through in your marketing strategy?

▶ What strategies could make the greatest impact in your business right now?

▶ If you can only focus on one initiative right now, what should it be?

▶ What do you need to do to ensure that you follow through on your marketing plan?

▶ Would it be helpful to recruit someone to keep you accountable?

▶ Would you like Sonnier Marketing to contact you in 30 days to give you an accountability check-in? If so, just e-mail us at lauron@sonniermarketing.com.

Tips 36–62 on How to Put Your Marketing Into Action

36. **Work events in three parts.** Any event such as a trade show or open house requires marketing before, during, and after the event. Before, it's all about building excitement and value to get targets there. During, it's about making impressions, building connections, and establishing a need or want for your offerings. After, it's about maintaining contact and moving

the relationship forward. Most people neglect one or more components, but each part becomes more effective with all three in place. Market events before, during, and after.

37. **Tell them what they missed.** A smart marketing move is to contact those who didn't attend your event (open house, trade show booth, Webinar, anything) to tell them what they missed. Show pictures and share all of the exciting highlights they would have enjoyed had they been there. They'll be sure to make it next time!

38. **Use different programs for different targets.** Not all targets are created equal, and that means different strategies for different groups. A-rated prospects may get extra attention with personal letters, calls, and visits in addition to the standard monthly mailings. B-level prospects may just get that monthly postcard while C-level prospects receive only e-mail blasts. This approach directs your resources to where they can serve you best while still allowing a broad reach of prospects. How can you qualify your targets? Devise a marketing strategy for each type.

39. **Head to the mall or sports arena for great marketing ideas.** Where else can you see so much marketing in one place? Walk around, look at everything, notice your reactions both good and bad, and of course, take notes.

40. **Hold on to inquiries.** It's a beautiful marketing moment when you get a prospect calling for information, but far too often he never gets past the receptionist who's too quick to answer his question and move on to the next incoming line. Establish a protocol for re-routing those inquiries to a salesperson. Those calls should be met with carefully devised questions to uncover any real business opportunities.

41. **Follow up after every contact.** Good contacts require good follow-up, so let them know how much you enjoyed meeting and talking to them. Send a short handwritten note. Make a call or drop a quick e-mail. Reference something from the conversation to refresh their memory and show you were paying attention. The follow-up can be more important than the original contact, so make it happen every time. And, of course add their name to your database to get them into your marketing program.

42. **Where else can you add information about your company?** When real estate agents attached a flyer tube to their for-sale yard signs, the quality of callers improved dramatically. Simple access to information serves you

and your customer. So where else does your information need to be? Outside your front door for after-hour visitors? At neighboring or related businesses where your customers also visit? Where else do you need to be to reach your target market? Think big and small.

43. **Give them a tool they can use.** A great way to remain in front of targets is to give them a helpful tool, something they will want to keep around such as a quick-reference guide, conversion table, tape measure, calendar, or industry-specific item. Choose something that makes sense for your business and helps you prove a marketing point.

44. **Do you need to educate your customer?** Can people easily understand what you offer at face value? Or, is it so specialized, technical, new, or extraordinary that they need to be educated about it? If so, a teaching component will be an important part of your marketing strategy and can be achieved through tip sheets, newsletters, articles, seminars, Webinars, instructional videos, and blogs. How much do you need to educate your customer about what you offer? How can you do that?

45. **Bring your company to life with video clips.** Get the camera rolling! Post short video clips on your Website and even other online avenues to get up close and personal with visitors. Welcome them to your site. Give tips or a tour of your facility. Demonstrate a product or explain a service. Feature customers giving personal testimonials about your company. Videos should be short and meaningful to your audience. Of course produce the best quality you can and make them easy to access and quick to download. Add links to your e-mails to drive traffic their way.

46. **Use wall space effectively.** Here's a place where you know you have visitors' attention, and that makes for another great marketing opportunity. Trade some of your lovely artwork for posters, photos, and text that market your company, introduce your team, and educate visitors about your business and what you can do for them. Everything is a canvas for marketing. And don't be afraid to pull out the paint. Add some color to make a statement. Just be sure it's consistent with your company's color scheme.

47. **Track activity to your Website and adjust your Web marketing accordingly.** You must know where visitors are going and where they're not so you can modify content and structure to work effectively for you. Extract and review Website activity reports at least monthly. (Add this to your Task Summary sheet.)

48. **Do a six-week marketing blast.** One way to get prospects' attention and make your marketing meaningful is to blast your message consistently for at least six weeks. Send postcards, letters, sample kits, specialty items, or a mix thereof in quick succession to build quick awareness. Then you can back down to a more relaxed schedule such as monthly. Consistency and frequency are essential, so don't be afraid to use even the same piece week after week. This technique is perfect when you're introducing yourself to a new market or when you really need a sales boost.

49. **Edit out bad processes.** As you work to create new processes for your marketing, take time to clean out those which could be counter-productive to your new program. "The way you've always done it" may not fit or serve you today, especially now that you're thinking like a marketer. Maybe it's time to face reality, make a tough decision, or take an undesirable action. If your instincts are telling you that something or someone needs to go, listen to them. Edit, edit, edit.

50. **Keep administrative details customer-friendly.** Your customers don't care about your data entry or filing system. They just want to be served well and quickly. Little frustrations like too many forms to fill out, too much time on hold, and too long to wait while you input personal information can be customer killers. Pay attention to every single administrative detail that touches the customer in any way. They are indeed important marketing tools.

51. **Incorporate social media into your daily routine.** There is an active community online, and it's not just for friendly chatters anymore. Your business associates, prospects, and competitors are connecting and conducting business through popular networking sites, and that means you need to be there, too. The cartoon with a man hugging his computer saying, "I love my computer because my friends are in it," tells it all. So show up, join the conversation, and put these social tools to work for you. Assign a champion and establish the protocols and routines to keep your business visible and talkative online. Just be sure you're contributing meaningful content to keep people interested and listening.

52. **Give advertising time to work.** People tend to expect too much from advertising too soon. First, choose your venues carefully. Get data and feedback to support your decision of where to advertise. Secondly, create an advertisement that stands out in the context where it will be competing. Make it look good, communicate something meaningful, and compel

the prospect to act. Then park it for a while. If you need to change content, do so but keep a consistent look. Once you've found a good venue, it's all about time and repetition. Be patient. Give your marketing time to work.

53. **Have at least one broad-brush tool working for you at all times.** As you develop your marketing plan, you likely will have various programs coming and going and targeting different audiences. In addition, choose one venue where you can stretch your reach to a broader universe on a consistent basis. It could be a well-placed advertisement, regular appearance on an Internet radio show, or a column in a trade industry newsletter— anything that regularly puts you in front of targets you would otherwise never be able to reach or find.

54. **Don't nitpick customers.** The devil is in the details, especially when money is concerned. Nobody enjoys the proverbial "nickel and dime treatment," yet companies dish it out all the time. Is it really right to charge for those last 15 minutes you spent correcting your own errors? Can't you just include that tiny item in the main cost? Couldn't you accept that expired coupon anyway? Never nitpick your customers. Be flexible, reasonable, and giving. Work with the big picture in mind.

55. **Don't make them do anything you could do for them.** Studies confirm that "being easy to work with" is one of the key factors that wins a customer and keeps a customer. Phrases such as "You can find that somewhere on our Website" or "Put it in the box outside" are dangerous. Instead, do the work for them. Save them the effort. Find the information they're asking about. Lead them to the product. Always make things easy for the customer. Demonstrate sincere willingness to help and give them the option of taking or leaving your assistance.

56. **Beware of policies that punish.** A growing trend is punishing customers with stiff late fees, shorter pay periods, tighter cancellation policies, and a host of other creative ways to add money to the bottom line. Beware! This "attack on customers" might put some extra dollars in the coffer, but the long-term effects could be detrimental. Don't treat customers as if they were children. Implement such policies if you must, but be reasonable and consider the long-term ramifications first.

57. **What customers are you losing and why?** You need to know, and that means you need a system to regularly monitor lost customers and their reasons for leaving. A good phone call is usually your best route to

understand what pulled a customer away and if revival is an option. Consider if an outside consultant would be useful to dig up honest answers. Document responses so you can identify trends and patterns that may require tactical changes in your business and marketing strategy.

58. **Mystery shop your own company.** Do it yourself or hire an expert, but one way or another, go undercover as an inquiring prospect or new customer. Dig up the good, the bad, the ugly, and the indifferent about your company. Get a firsthand look at how it performs on the hot seat. Test it from every angle. The only way to truly know what a customer or prospect experiences is to become one.

59. **Never make customers wait if there's a warm body around.** You know the scene. As a customer, you've most assuredly been there—standing in a growing checkout line waiting, watching, and wondering why employees are buzzing around you doing everything else but taking care of you. Never let this happen! Everyone should know how to serve the customer and that serving the customer trumps all other duties, especially when they're trying to pay you!

60. **Keep track of common customer questions, complaints, and frustrations.** Establish a system to capture and respond to them immediately throughout your organization.

61. **Put your logo and contact information on everything.** Toilet paper may be the only exception. If there is a document, instrument, or tool that represents you, it must prominently contain your logo and contact information. Every page, every part, every product, everything! This means your Website, too. When a visitor prints out any page, she should have all of the information she needs to contact you the old fashioned way. Take a look around your business. Where else do you need to add your logo and contact information?

62. **Have professional photos taken.** Put your best image forward with professionally produced photos. They are definitely worth every penny. Just be sure to use current images. You don't want anyone being startled when they meet you because you've gained 30 pounds or 30 years since your last photo. (This is the literal translation of keeping your image and identity in sync.) Then, get those photos out there. Put your photo on your Website and even consider it for your business card. People like to see and know whom they're dealing with. So call the photographer and put a smile on!

SMAC Marketing Plan Detail™

Goal (#)	Target	Strategy	Action	Champion	Time/Schedule	Measurement	Budget

SMAC Marketing Plan Detail™

Sample

Goal (#)	Target	Strategy	Action	Champion	Time/Schedule	Measurement	Budget
Be a marketing-minded company	EEs	Produce a written marketing role of each staff member	Each employee submit his/her ideas of marketing role; each collaborate with manager to establish final description	Each employee; senior managers	EE notes due 2/08; finalize by 3/16	N/A	None
		Conduct marketing foundation training for all staff levels	Choose instructor; develop agenda; schedule date; determine plan for training new hires	Marketing director; HR manager; president	March	Behavior and performance after training; customer ratings	$_____ for trainer
		Establish ongoing marketing awareness and "impressions improvement program"	Hold "marketing moments" in monthly staff meetings; create marketing bulletin board; create incentive for great impressions	Marketing director; president	Monthly	Perceived mindfulness and improvement to marketing actions; feedback	None
		Build strong knowledge about the company among staff; educate team how to promote, cross-promote, and up-sell	Each department to conduct educational sessions; determine common service points and develop action plans; develop company answers to common customer questions	President; department managers	Action plans and questions by 4/1; begin educational sessions by 4/15	Evidence of learning in action; test given after training	None

Task Summary   *Sample*

Daily	Champion
Make great impressions	All
Ask, *What is the marketing opportunity here?*	All

Weekly

Run report of new customers	Accounts receivable
Send welcome kit to new customers	Marketing director
Update company databases	Marketing assistant
Hold marketing and sales collaboration meetings	Marketing and sales teams
Update marketing calendar & bulletin board	Marketing director
Conduct at least 5 prospect calls	Sales team, president

Monthly

Review inactive customers and implement protocol	Sales director
Send e-zine to customers and prospects	Marketing director
Send direct mail vehicle to targets	Marketing director
Present "marketing moments" at staff meeting	All
Review website activity reports	Marketing director
Attend industry organization meetings	Marketing and sales team
Conduct instructional webinar; send e-blast to promote next month's topic	Marketing/departments

Bi-Monthly

Review all marketing tracking systems and make necessary adjustments in plan	Marketing director

Quarterly

Review advertising plan	Marketing director
Produce and send tip sheets to all targets	Marketing director

Annually

Hold company open house	All
Send personal thank you to all customers	President

Marketing Calendar *Sample*

Month 1
• Develop company's graphic standards manual
• Develop 6-part postcard campaign for key targets
• Write staff marketing roles
• Mastermind and devise company's "Marketing Machine" campaign
• Devise and begin production on New Customer Welcome Packet; schedule photo shoot for individual and group photos
• Hold team planning session to develop company's List of Attributes, identify service points, and develop response protocols

Month 2
• Send postcard campaign to print
• Mail first prospect postcard by 15th
• Launch company-wide "Marketing Machine" campaign; conduct one-on-one meetings with staff to discuss their individual marketing roles
• Go to print on Welcome Packet components by the 25th
• Develop new template and topic list for bi-weekly e-mail blasts
• Develop idea list for company press releases

Month 3
• Mail prospect postcard on 1st and 15th
• Conduct instructional webinar for customers; send e-mail blast promotion for next month's topic
• Launch bi-weekly e-mail blast program by 21st
• Conduct thorough company audit of standard marketing opportunities in the day-to-day operation of business
• Begin call program of minimum of five prospect calls per week

Month 4
• Mail prospect postcard on 1st and 15th
• Devise company contest to uncover indifferent impressions
• Conduct brainstorming sessions with each department to improve their respective marketing impact
• Begin development of media database
• Reserve space for tradeshow

Month 5
• Mail prospect postcard on 1st and 15th
• Make at least three improvements in turning indifferent impressions into great impressions
• Update Website with new staff photos and bios
• Develop press releases on new equipment and staff additions
• Write annual customer thank you letter

Month 6
• Shift prospect postcard campaign to 3-week rotation beginning on the 1st
• Make 3 more "great" improvements in the business
• Send company press releases and make phone follow-ups
• Order specialty advertising items for tradeshow
• Begin developing annual customer survey
• Send personalized customer thank you letters

Talk Like a Marketer

It's not just what you say, but how you say it that counts.

Chapter 15

How You Say It

Standing out with your words

Marketers like to talk and they have a lot to say. But like everything else in marketing, it's not just what you do, but how you do it that counts.

My mother unwittingly taught me a second important marketing lesson. Just as often as she was telling me to stir the pot, she was saying, "Lauron, it's not what you say, but how you say it that gets you in trouble." (Mama was very wise.)

Companies cause a lot of trouble every day by saying the wrong thing or saying nothing at all. Every day I cringe at the verbal clumsiness and ineptitude of the business world. Poor communication skills run amuck like pesky bacteria polluting relationships, tarnishing reputations, and killing opportunities.

Marketers know better. Marketers understand that words, and how they are delivered, matter. Words can move mountains. Words can build egos and destroy nations. They can separate a man from his money and a woman from her heart.

Words have energy. They have weight and personality. They can turn heads and paint intricate pictures, or do absolutely nothing. They can rest on a page or waltz a prospect right to your door.

All of your external marketing comes down to what you say and how you say it. Whatever form your communications take—paper, e-mail, ad, presentation, Website, blog, video, podcast, whatever—you have to make a statement that will cut through the clutter and make your voice heard. Then it must move others to act. With your words, you must duplicate yourself and your business onto a cold piece of paper or digital file in a way that will get noticed, stir emotions, make great impressions, and motivate targets to do whatever you want them to do. Choose your words carelessly and you waste marketing time, dollars, and opportunities. Choose them well and you can make magic happen.

Words are powerful indeed, and they usually don't require many syllables to make their impact. Consider these:

- Will you marry me?
- I hate you.
- No.
- Yes.
- I'm pregnant.
- Don't drink the water.
- Get it free.
- There's been an accident.
- It's gone.
- I have great news for you.
- I have bad news for you.
- You won't believe what I just heard.

- You're hired.
- You're fired.
- Fire!
- She married an engineer.
- I danced with John Travolta.
- Do you trust me?
- We're at war.
- He's dead.
- She had the baby.
- She won.
- We lost.
- They bought it.
- We got the deal.

Certainly context always matters, but these short statements alone create strong feelings and vivid pictures. Just reading them to yourself gets the emotions stirring.

That's exactly what you must do in your marketing. You must use your words to move, motivate, engage, provoke, stir, direct, connect, break in, break through, and stand out from the pack.

Communicating like a marketer is a life skill. It will serve you with any target audience anywhere for any purpose. And it's easy, when you know a few techniques. Sometimes the slightest change can turn boring into exhilarating and insignificant into important. As a marketer, you must know how to construct your words for great impact. As a marketing machine, your team must know as well.

What is said and communicated every day in your company can bolster or unravel your marketing in an instant. One mindless slip of the tongue can create a world of damage and wreck years of hard marketing. That means every time an employee opens his mouth or writes anything, your company has both opportunity and risk. You can make great impressions, get stuck in indifference, or kill relationships. As the "impressions police," you must keep your ears open and attuned to all messages coming from your company in any way.

In the end, what you say and how you say it must be the culmination and manifestation of all of your strategic planning. All of the other hard work you do is lost if you cannot communicate effectively with your targets. Words are the tools that help marketing ideas take flight, so apply what you learn here and continually supplement your knowledge and hone your communication and writing skills, personally and as a company. Look around and pay attention to all of the words that surround you in this mass-marketed world. Take note of what moves you and what doesn't so you can apply that knowledge in your own messaging.

Even if you are not the resident marketing writer, you must be able to direct the process of executing powerful marketing messages. The skill set of a professional writer is different than that of a professional marketing writer. You must know and be able to identify the difference.

So, now that you're thinking like a marketer and acting like a marketer, it's time to learn how to communicate like one. Fortunately, there are some smart techniques to help you move mountains, stir emotions, and stand out in a noisy, ill-spoken marketplace.

In this Phase, I will address some of the key concepts you need to be thinking about as you develop your marketing messages and materials. I'll give you a secret formula to writing a killer marketing letter. And, I'll give you an extra serving of tips to make you talk and communicate like a marketing pro.

How You Say It

Communicating like a marketer encompasses careful strategy and construction in both your message and its presentation. You must pay attention to every detail—the words used, the tone in which they are delivered, and the physical packaging in which they are presented. Everything counts. Everything adds or takes away from their meaning and impact.

In verbal communications, tone of voice is often more important than the actual words used and can actually change or determine the meaning of your words. For example, if you told someone, "Get out of here," it would be your tone that would clarify whether you were exclaiming disbelief about something you just heard, or if you really did want someone to leave the room.

In business, the wrong tone can quickly turn communications sour, especially in e-mails where there is no audible assistance to manage the message. With e-mail now being the primary means of communication, it is ever more important that everyone be trained on effective writing skills. One easy solution is to make sure all e-mails begin and end with a pleasantry such as, "Hope this finds you well" and "I look forward to hearing from you soon." If that seems out of place for the content of the e-mail, then perhaps a phone call would be a better choice of delivery.

The literal packaging of your message is also of great importance. A message in a large red envelope says something different than one folded in a standard size envelope, or a folder, or a tube, or a CD. Colors and paper textures set a mood and make a statement. Again, everything matters. Every detail either bolsters your overall message or diminishes it.

How words sit on a page or computer screen affect how they are read. The placement, size, and typestyle of your text set a tone and personality for the message. With a few clicks of the mouse, type can scream at targets or whisper with understated elegance, and everything in between.

You would think that any graphic artist would understand this since so much of what they produce is for marketing purposes. Don't assume such. Just as all writers are not marketing writers, all designers do not think like a marketer. All the time I see "professionally produced" and beautifully printed marketing pieces and extra flashy Websites that I know cost the value of my car, and yet the words and overall message are lost because the design overdominates them. The words and the central point or idea become almost an afterthought to the design.

Words are always part of the design. The words are not secondary, but the focus, the starting point, and the lasting impression. The design's purpose is to get the words noticed. It should enforce and enhance the content being delivered. Too often companies get this backward, sending a graphic designer off to create a masterpiece, with the words just thrown in as a last step. It must be the other way around. Believe me, I love slick graphic designs, but even the simplest of designs and cheapest of papers can be successful marketing tools if the message is strong enough. As a marketer in control, you must work your words first and then build your design around them.

When selecting outside professionals to help you develop your messages and materials, be sure you're working with true experts. Ask to read and view several samples of their work. Ask about their philosophy and approach to making a marketing piece successful. You will find many types of people producing marketing materials. Some are artists, some are software experts, and some are true marketers. In whatever combination you assemble between you and them, be sure you have *all* of those skills working for you.

The Mindset

As usual, if you work from the right mindset, you can figure out the details as you go. Keep these critical factors in mind as you develop your marketing messages and materials:

1. **In the minds of your targets, your marketing tools don't just represent you, they *are* you.** Until targets experience your company personally, they will formulate their impressions and perceptions of you based on your outside "stuff" such as your brochure, business card, and Website. These paper and digital messages must be walking, talking, and breathing replicas of your company. They must do, say, and be all that you would if you were sitting in the flesh directly in front of your target every time. Your brochure is you on paper. Your Website is you online. How they look and how they function are perceivably how you look and function everywhere else. The adjectives targets would use to describe those tools would be how they would describe you. If your brochure is lame and boring, then you are lame and boring. If your Website is fun and happening, then you are fun and happening. There is no separation. You are your stuff, so make it good. Make it right.

2. **Everything is marketing, so everything matters.** Every aspect of every communication makes an impression and creates a perception that must be accurate, helpful, and most of all, consistent. Again, every detail impacts the overall message you send—colors, paper textures, paper weight, font styles, design, message, tone, how your words sit on the page—every single thing. Do not let the excuse of budget hold you back. Of course it's easier to make ultimate impressions when you have an open budget, but that doesn't mean you can't make a great impression on a small one. I've spent most of my career making big impacts on tight budgets, so I know it can be done. Sometimes there will be sacrifices. Instead of the slick embossed and foil-stamped folder, you might have to go with one off the shelf. Sometimes

> *Do not let what you cannot do interfere with what you can do.*
>
> —John Wooden

there will just be choices. If you want to communicate that you're a company of solidity and strength, you will definitely want to use a paper stock that is noticeably thicker than what's commonly used. That's just a matter of paying attention and asking, *How can we make a great impression here?*

Do the best you can with what you have, but watch details and make calculated choices. Don't just go with the wind and complain that you don't have enough money to do it right. Never before have the opportunities for obtaining high quality in small quantities of just about anything been more available. With the proliferation of small businesses and leaping advancements in technology, your options are plenty, even on a budget. Dig around, be mindful, and choose strategically.

3. **The words you use day-to-day in your business are some of the most important marketing you do.** How you answer the telephone, interact with customers, answer questions, and generally conduct every step of business is all driven by words: words on paper, words on signs, words out of mouth, and words in an e-mail or posted online. Words, words, words. And what goes around comes around. If you give great words to your targets, they will give great words back. Give them poor words, and they will definitely have some words for you.

All this means that you will need to pay close attention to what your company is saying every day in everything it does. You will need to take time to carefully construct answers to common questions. You will need to have great discipline in training and monitoring staff so they are moving your marketing and business forward with their mouths. This is critical. Staff can hurt you and help you all day by what they say and how they say it. Giving everyone in your team the opportunity, and the expectancy, of learning and practicing smart communication skills makes business better for everyone. You cannot be a marketing machine unless everyone talks like a marketer. Fortunately for you, I have more than a few words to help you.

Are You Talking to Me?

What would you say is the most important word in marketing? No, it's not "free," though that one can definitely be powerful.

Look around and give the marketplace a good listen. The most popular word seems to be "we." *We're the best. We're number one. We've been in business forever. We have the best prices. We're better than the other guy. We're your end-all, be-all.*

"We" is overdone. Sometimes it's annoying, and often it can be costly as people work to build themselves up only to have targets turn away because they didn't communicate in a meaningful or relevant manner. As a buyer, when I hear all of those "we" statements, I'm just thinking, *I don't care.* I don't care how long you've been in business. I don't care how great you are. Whatever you're saying makes no difference to me whatsoever. Zero. Zip. In fact, I'm wondering if you're talking to me at all. That is, if I'm taking the time to think anything at all.

People don't like to listen to people who only talk about themselves. If that's what you do, people won't want to listen to you either. There must be a conversation, a back and forth exchange with targets where sometimes you talk and sometimes you listen. That means using the most important word in marketing: *you.*

Something magical happens when we hear the word *you.* Our ears perk up. If the tone is pleasant, we become engaged and we listen. If the tone is even slightly negative, we bow up and get ready to defend ourselves. But we always, always pay attention.

Companies need to stop talking *at* targets and start talking *with* them. That means using the all-powerful word *you* to get attention, bring targets into the conversation, and lead them to a positive outcome.

Getting From "We" to "You"

There is a reason why "we" is so popular. First, people tend to think of themselves first; that's only natural. Secondly, it's a logical approach. How can we market ourselves without talking about ourselves?

There's where the thinking goes askew. Remember, marketing is not about you. It's about your target. Therefore, your communications must be about your target. That's why "you" is the most important word, because it's the one that matters most to every target.

Although you are using the most important word, you should also be answering the most important question—*What's in it for me?* Now talking like a marketer becomes a lot easier. You can't answer the most important question without using the most important word. When you switch your focus to your target, you get out of the "we syndrome" and into a state that will get your message heard. Which of these statements would more likely get your attention?

We have been in business for 30 years so we are skilled and experienced to deliver the best product possible.

or

You can relax knowing that your job will be done accurately because we've been perfecting our skills for 30 years.

See the tremendous difference when you simply change perspectives? Hands down, the second sentence has much greater impact. You can feel it as you read it. Notice also the emotion word *relax* strategically inserted there. With that little addition, the entire tone of the message changes. Now the customer is not only getting accuracy because of the company's 30-year experience, she's also getting the ability to relax. When the competition starts talking about how great they are and how they've been in business for 40 years, do you think it's going to matter? Absolutely not. With this company, the customer gets to relax, and what customer wouldn't want that?

Another little jewel to help you go from "we" to "you" is the use of a bridging statement such as:

That means for you...

Because we do this, you can...

To help you, we...

So you can...

So you get...

Example:	With our new job tracking system, you can manage your job online quickly and easily, 24/7.
Even Better:	You'll love our new job tracking system. With it, you can manage your job online quickly and easily, 24/7.
A Couple More:	Because we hire only certified technicians, you can trust that your car will be fixed right—and done in a reasonable amount of time.
	We include all of the tools so you'll have everything you need right there, right then.

Before considering any communication finished, especially an ad, sales letter, direct mail piece, or your Website, give it a quick check to make sure your "we-you ratio" is in good balance. Scan it for places to add punch and impact by changing a sentence around or adding a bridging statement.

We, I, and They

When you do need to talk about yourself, the word *we* is not only acceptable, it's your best bet. If you are to act as a company, you must present yourself as a company. You can't do that with individuals walking around using "I" when they should be saying "we."

I wince every time I hear a waiter tell me what she is offering me for dinner. You know how it goes. "I have for you tonight a grilled salmon and this luscious sauce that is sure to stick to your thighs." As a business owner, that frustrates me. The waiter does not have anything for me except maybe a smile and hopefully some great service. Everything else belongs to the company. The waiter does not pay for the salmon or take the hit when the salmon goes bad.

If, in the mind of the customer, every individual in the company *is* the company, then everyone must operate from a "we" standpoint. *We have many wonderful options for you tonight. We're so happy you joined us. We have some questions about your job.* Each and all team members *are* the company, so each and all team members must operate with a "we" mentality.

There are some situations when "I" is appropriate, such as when an individual needs to explain what that one individual is or will be doing. *I will call you the second it's ready. I'm going to leave this at the counter.*

The other main time when "I" is most appropriate is when responsibility needs to be taken, such as when there is an error that is clearly the fault of one and only one person. *I apologize. I misunderstood. I mis-communicated that to our printing department.*

Great caution must be taken when using "they." It is always appropriate to give "them" credit for a job well done, but "they" should never be blamed when things go wrong. Expressions like, *They made a mistake,* must be strictly discouraged. Instead, one could say, *It looks like an error was made at that point of the process. We will fix that right away.* Problems are always best discussed in terms of actions, not people.

"We" is always a safe default when talking about your company, in good news and in bad. Tread lightly when using "I" or "they."

What's In It for Me?

This topic is so significant that it deserves and requires a little more discussion. Every conversation with your target in print, in person, and otherwise, must tell your target what's in it for him. The more you practice communicating from this standpoint, the more natural it will become. Your target is always consciously or subconsciously asking why he should choose you, pay you, trust you, listen to you, whatever.

If you want your target to buy from you, tell him what's in it for him if he does. If you want him to give you another day to do the job, spend extra money, anything, tell him what's in it for him. Whatever product, service, or idea you're marketing, you have to tell your target what's in it for him, and that means you have to get clear on what that is.

> *If you buy this product, you will cut your production costs by 25 percent or more.*
>
> *If you mail that back to me today, we will still be able to make your deadline.*
>
> *Thank you for being so thorough in your specifications. It helps us to get started on your job faster and eliminate the possibility of errors along the way.*

Could you firmly tell your targets right now what's in it for them to do business with you? Could your entire team?

The real skill comes in being specific. General, vague, surface answers are what everyone gives and they don't say anything. There's nothing there to discern you as a better choice. Keep drilling down to the real details that matter. When you think you've gone as deep as you can go, ask what that means for the customer and see if you can dig a little more. Think about the real estate agent who just wants to say she'll sell your house fast and at a good price. She's saying what everyone says, but the target has a ton of other questions that could make or break the deal. You're likely not telling your story in a manner as deep or as rich as you could. Keep digging and keep telling your targets what's in it for them.

Getting Specific

In getting down to the details that matter to your target and that will make your message interesting and meaningful, you have to continually ask that all-powerful question, *What does that mean for the customer?* Let's look at an example of how you can use this question to get down to the real message you should be communicating.

You say: Mr. Prospect, you should hire us because we're the best accounting firm in town.

Customer thinks: So what?

What does that mean for the customer?

You say: We have great expertise, lots of experience, and are focused on customer service.

Customer thinks: I like that, but that's what everyone says. Tell me something new. What's really in it for me?

What does that mean for the customer?

You say: Mr. Customer, you can rest assured that your tax return will be done accurately and that you will receive the maximum deductions possible. Plus, you're going to love working with us.

Customer thinks: Now I'm listening. You're worth considering.

What does that mean for the customer?

You say: You just give us your raw data and we'll handle everything from there. We will conduct a double review to ensure that you're getting every advantage allowed by law. You can feel certain that your tax return will be completely accurate and that we will handle any questions or issues brought up by the IRS for you. We will keep you informed every step of the way, and we'll remain available to you throughout the year to give you guidance anytime you need it.

Customer thinks: Wow, that's exactly what I want in an accounting firm. You're hired!

As a customer, I'm sure you can relate to this type of example. As a marketer, you know that you must constantly refine your message to drill deeper and deeper into the real issues that matter to your target. Remember that people buy the process as much as the product. Targets are just as concerned with the how as the what. And, they don't care about you—only what you can do for them.

As you develop your marketing messages and materials, keep asking the question, *What does that mean for the customer?* Every time you ask it, you step farther and farther out of the gray until you become something special, different, and extraordinary—and you make money.

Know-Think-Feel-Do

This handy tool should be a staple for you. You may even want to make a simple form that you can pull out anytime to note and clarify answers before plunging into a marketing piece. With each one, ask these simple but powerful questions to help you discern the best direction for your message:

As a result of this communication,

> *What do I want the target to **know** about us?*
>
> *What do I want the target to **think** about us?*
>
> *What do I want the target to **feel** about us?*
>
> *What do I want the target to **do**?*

Once you have your own answers, you will need to explore answers from your target's perspective to make sure you are aligned in telling your target what really matters to her. So ask:

For my target to be motivated to do as I am asking:

> *What does my target need to **know** about us?*
>
> *What does my target need to **think** about us?*
>
> *What does my target need to **feel** about us?*

All of these answers will help you organize and determine the specific content that is sure to make your message meaningful, masterful, and successful.

Say It Like You Mean It

As a marketer, you must be confident in what you are marketing, and that must ring through in your communications. How often do we receive marketing communications overwrought with wimpy words like hope, maybe, perhaps, hesitate, and problem? Emotions are contagious. When you are weak in your words, targets will be weak in their response. No one wants to give money to someone who isn't overjoyed to take it. Yet, all the time, we are exposed to messages that, in effect, say, "I hope you will like my product and maybe, perhaps you might like to buy it, too." It seems silly looking at it here, but I hear that from lots of people who call themselves marketers.

Put some weight in your words. Whatever your point, say it like you mean it. Be strong and concise. Instead of saying "we hope" you will, say "we're confident" or "we're certain" you will. Instead of saying "call at your earliest convenience," say "call right now."

If you are strong, upbeat, and convinced in your words, your targets will be, too. If you create a sense of urgency, they'll act faster. That's why you must never ever commit the cardinal sin of saying, "Don't hesitate." You've just subconsciously told them to hesitate.

Research has proved that the brain does not process the word "not." If you tell yourself not to eat the donut, all your brain hears is donut and you start craving one. Therefore, we must send clear, direct messages to our brain about what we do want instead of the things we don't want. Same goes for your targets. If you don't want your targets to hesitate, never use the word. If you want targets to call right away, tell them to call right away and tell them what's in it for them to do it.

Always write and speak in strong, active, positive terms. An over-used expression is, "Our goal is..." Criminals have goals. Millions of people have goals on January 1 to lose weight. We use the expression all the time, but does it really mean anything? Goals are about the future; your targets want to know what you're doing for them right now. Instead of talking about your goal, tell targets what you're doing right now or what you "work hard every day" to do for them.

After you get your words down in any communication, cull through them once, twice, even three times to change negative to positive, inactive to active, and wimpy to hefty. The difference is enormous. Compare the following statements:

> *We hope you will find our service to be acceptable and we look forward to hearing from you at your earliest convenience. Please do not hesitate to call if I can answer any questions for you.*

> *We are certain you will find our service to be a prudent method for ensuring the accuracy and expediency of your accounting. Please contact us right away to get started. I am available to you at 555-5555 or around the clock at me@mywebsite.com. We look forward to working hard and doing a great job for you!*

Let's do a little dissection. Notice the many wimpy words in the first example: hope, acceptable, convenience, hesitate. When you single them out like this, it's easy to see how much they weaken your overall message. "Acceptable" is hardly a glowing recommendation for your offering. The target is being asked to call whenever he can get around to it. We're suggesting that he hesitate and implying that he might have something to question. Are you feeling motivated? I'm certainly not. The energy level alone gets a low score. It's average language, but not marketing language.

Now let's extract key words from the second example: certain, prudent, accuracy, expediency, right away, get started, available, around the clock, working hard, doing a great job. It's a very different message. It stresses urgency and makes acting easy with the contact information right there. It re-emphasizes benefits and tells him what's it in for him (accuracy, expediency, working hard, great job). It relays strong emotions with certain, prudent, and around the clock. This one cranks up the energy, the confidence, and the motivation. What was standard, boring, drab correspondence became an interesting, affirming, and energizing marketing message.

Pull out the key words and expressions in your writing to help you see the real strength of your message.

Kill the Marketing-Speak

When you see a sign or billboard that reads, *The Best Restaurant in Town*, what does that really say to you? Sweeping statements like that try to boost credibility when, in actuality, they just diminish it. People are argumentative. They like finding loopholes. Who says you're the best? Best of what kind of restaurant? Does that mean best food or best service or both?

How about this one: "We are the leaders in innovative technologies and state-of-the-art solutions that exceed your expectations and meet all of your needs." What the heck does that mean? It must be something really impressive because so-called marketers say it all the time.

It's time to kill the marketing-speak and say something real. Stop worrying about using the latest buzzwords and just tell people what you do. Be clever. Be original like the dog groomers in my neighborhood whose sign says, *We Bathe Stinky Puppies.* It's simple and direct and much more interesting than just saying they're dog groomers.

As a busy person, I definitely appreciate when marketers just come out and say what needs to be said. "We sell insurance." There's nothing to be confused about there. If I don't need insurance, I don't need to look at the card. If I do, I give it a read. If I have to dig or think too much to understand what the company is trying to tell me, I'm out of there. I'm already loving companies who don't waste my time.

Bad marketing-speak is everywhere. Its intentions are good, but its execution is poor and a real waste of a marketing opportunity. Be real. Be direct. Be specific. Tell them what you want them to do. Get rid of the clutter and the litter in your marketing messages. Get rid of hollow and empty phrases such as *quality service, state-of-the-art,* and *all of your needs.* Just talk to your targets as though they were sitting across the table from you and tell them outright what they need to know, think, and feel about your business, and what you want them to do. Simple and straightforward is always well-received and usually more effective.

Stir Emotions

Too many communications are stuck in an emotional gray zone. Your words must provoke, move, and sensitize your products and services. They must make your company and the benefits of choosing your company come to life. So, again, be simple and straightforward. Just come out and tell targets how you want them to feel. If you want a target to love something, tell her she's going to love it and then tell her why. If you want your target to feel confident, use the word *confident* and then list all the reasons why he will feel that way. Talk about emotions and back them up with facts. That's how targets make choices and decisions anyway, so speak directly to their thinking process. Detailed descriptions, vivid pictures, stories, examples, customer testimonials, and case studies are always productive tools in stirring emotions. However you need to do it, get your targets feeling good!

Sell It With Headlines

Headlines sell newspapers and they will sell your marketing message. Marketers think in headlines and we use them everywhere—on our direct mail marketing letters, Websites, fax cover sheets, internal posters, trade show exhibits, brochures, everywhere.

Headlines can quickly stir emotions and distill a big concept into a few words. They help you lead every communication with a bang, and that is mandatory if you are to get a target's attention in a noisy marketplace. Strong headlines make targets take notice and then think, question, become curious, and read on.

The headline is one of the marketer's best friends. The rest of the world, on the other hand, likes labels and puts them everywhere. Fax Cover Sheet. Registration Form. Response Card. Not so exciting and certainly not as effective.

One of the gravest errors in this area is the brochure. People use labels on the primary tool they use to inform and attract targets. Brochures absolutely need a headline! There is nothing motivating or exciting about Product Listing or Services List. It's better than nothing, but it can be trumped many times over with a strong headline. Labels are strictly utilitarian, indifferent, and wasted marketing opportunities. Use them freely when organizing the supply closet. For everything else, use a headline. Kick up the labels with colorful language or add an action word. For example:

Label	Headline
Fax Cover Sheet	*Important Fax from Your Favorite Contractor*
Registration Form	*Count Me In!*
Response Card	*Yes, I would love to know how I can get a free design consultation. Tell me more.*
Services List	*We Make Your Home Beautiful in Every Way*
Discounts up to 50%	*Save 50% Today*

As you develop a variety of marketing materials, you will find countless opportunities for headlines. There are only rare exceptions and, at the moment, I can't think of any. I use headlines everywhere, even in a standard business letter and simple e-mail. I may not set the words to look exactly like a headline, but I usually make the first sentence larger or bolder than the rest of the body type.

Force yourself to think in headlines. It will dramatically increase the effectiveness of your communications and make you and your message stand out. If you opened a letter, e-mail, or anything else to find a statement like the ones below, wouldn't you want to keep reading?

Don't drink the water.

You aren't going to believe what we're doing now.

I have great news for you.

What a delight to meet you!

Save 50% when you hurry in Saturday.

You're going to want to call me the second you finish this letter.

Life insurance costs much less than you think.

Do you feel pain with your current dentist?

Here are 10 new ways to save a ton of money each month.

This is the most important thing you'll hear all day.

Is your delivery service treating you like a king?

Imagine sitting on the beach right now.

Remember the thrill of your first car?

Several things are happening in this list. Some headlines stir feelings and emotions, both good and bad. Some provoke curiosity or a need to act. Some engage the target to enter or recall another time or place. All of them get the target thinking.

Just like the list at the beginning of this chapter, these short, punchy statements stir emotions and make people want to read on. It's the headline that can get your entire piece read, so give it a good one.

Answering the Know-Think-Feel-Do questions will help you know what to do with your headlines. Then make them quick, direct, and heavy-hitting. Targets may read nothing but the headline, so tell them what you would want them to know if they read nothing else! Oddly enough, that is the very thing that will make them want to read more.

Call in the Subs

When you have a lengthy communication like a proposal, brochure, or long direct mail letter, you will need to break up your text with sub-headings. These are your best tools for organizing your content and gliding the reader through your text. The key rule about sub-headings is that they should be consistent in their tone throughout the piece, and they should reinforce the theme established in the headline. If you start the first sub-heading with a verb, then start each one that way.

Ideally, your sub-headings should tell a story. For example, if you started a piece with the headline, "You're Going to Love Working With Us," then you could begin all of your sub-headings with "You'll Love" such as "You'll Love the Convenience" and "You'll Love the Price."

Not every marketing piece will present the same opportunity to be so smooth, but in all cases, the reader should be able to extract the headline and the sub-headings only and be able to understand the essential gist of your message. Best yet, the reader will understand some of the benefits and reasons to say yes.

End All Communications With a Call to Action

Every single communication must absolutely end with a call to action—every flyer, ad, brochure, Website page, proposal, estimate, everything. Tell your targets to call, write, mail, e-mail, visit, consider, choose, buy, order, submit, fax, click, whatever. No piece is finished until it tells the target what to do next.

Create Urgency

While you have your target's attention, you need to make the most of it by encouraging him to move quickly. You may never have another chance, or he may talk himself out of it if there's any delay. That's why you see everywhere, "Call now. Operators are standing by. Call in the next 10 minutes and receive this $18,000 value for just $9.99." As a marketer, you must be quick to act and you must encourage your targets to do the same. Review all of your marketing messages. Do you need to entice targets with an incentive or deadline? The world operates by the clock, and so should your marketing.

Make Your Communications Scannable

Pick up a magazine and the first thing you'll likely do is scan the headlines, sub-headings, large quotes, sidebars, and boxed items—all of the things that stand out. It's a smart way to discern whether reading the entire article is worthy of your precious time. Being aware of this behavior confirms that you must make your own communications scannable. This means that, at a quick glance—without really reading anything—your target must be able to understand the general gist of your message and be able to determine that the rest is worth reading.

Headlines and sub-headlines are marketing gold in this respect. They definitely make a piece scannable, as well as bold text, underlines, and type set in a different size, color, or style. You can also use bullet lists, write in short paragraphs, and use white space wisely to direct eyes to your message. Beware of wall-to-text which is a true sign of an amateur designer. Keep margins clean and comfortable. Too much text and too little white space make a reader overwhelmed and quick to look away.

Take a look at the marketing materials you're using right now—just look at them. Do certain things stand out? Do they make an important marketing point? If that's all the information your reader took from that piece, would she generally understand who you are, what you do, and what you're offering? Would she have reason to act? Make every marketing communication scannable.

Don't Be Afraid of Long Copy

It is generally accepted that the more expensive, more technical, and more intangible a product or service, the more you may need to say about it to help the target justify or understand the purchase. Some marketers are still raking in tons of money with 24-page direct mail letters set in basic courier type because the writing is really strong. It is perfectly acceptable to be long-winded as long as your content is relevant and meaningful, and as long as it moves quickly. Organization is key. Say what needs to be said, short or long, and then get out of there. If there is a tremendous amount to be said, consider if it would be better told in stages to keep targets mindful.

What's Your Point?

You cannot tell a target everything about you in any one communication, so stop trying. Make one key point in each communication. You can and likely should have several points to support your statement, but all content must support one central idea, one key concept. Your headline sets this up for you. It becomes your theme, and everything from there should enforce and reinforce that theme. That makes for a strong marketing message, and one your target can take away easily and clearly. Make your point and stick to it.

Establish Graphic and Communication Standards

People make marketing complicated by not making decisions. When it comes to your graphics and communications, you need to decide the standards by which all things are to be designed, developed, and created. Print colors, Web colors, typestyles, design guidelines, use of the logo. Make your choices and get them in writing. You cannot have a consistent look and message with everybody doing their own thing and starting from scratch each time. Make your choices. Get them in writing. Inform everyone involved and hold them to your new standards. Your work will be much easier and your end product more effective.

Be Consistent

There are many ways to apply the principles of consistency in the production of marketing materials. You need consistency across the board and within each specific piece.

Trouble happens when people work in singles instead of bulk, which is usually what occurs. Let's take postcards, for example. If you determine a postcard campaign to be a wise initiative for your business, then there are ways to greatly enhance your chances for success while making the process easier on your time and your budget.

To do this, you must work in campaigns instead of single cards. Decide a theme and build several postcards at once to carry out your theme. Develop your graphic look and content flow one time and then repurpose for each card. It's easy for you, and it creates the consistency you need to make an impact with targets. Even if targets take it to the trashcan, they'll be able to identify the message as yours once they've been exposed to the same look a few times. They'll know it's you even without reading it. Another benefit to this method is that you can print all of your pieces at once, thereby getting bulk rates on your printing. Everything will be ready to grab off the shelf when it's time to send out each piece. Marketing becomes automatic, stress-free, and more successful because you are consistent in message, presentation, and timing.

Say It With Pictures—or Video

The proliferation of video online has raised the standard for the sensory demands of our buyers. We want an up close and personal view of people and the things we buy. And, for the most part, it's all there, even to the extent of looking in someone's backyard via satellite. Always consider how you can bring your product, service, and your marketing point to life with pictures and videos. They aren't just advantageous anymore; they're expected.

Tell Them What You Do, Not Just What You Are

That illustrious and ever-popular question, "What do you do?" often throws people into a tailspin. I've struggled with that one myself. Too often people throw around nebulous terms that they and only they understand. Computer consultant. Success advisor. What do those really mean? What do those people really do? At face value, no one knows. If you are an accountant, that does make things much easier, but that alone doesn't tell me everything I might need to know about you—or know why you're different or better than the rest.

That question again is, "What do you do?" It's not, "What are you?" You will need to practice and test your official introduction so you can make the most of that marketing opportunity when someone actually asks and wants to hear about what you do. Your goal always is to be specific and clear so people know at face value why they need to talk to you, learn more about you, consider your offerings, and tell others about you. Here's a handy formula for coming up with your big answer to the big question:

I/we do what, for whom, how (benefit).

I teach entrepreneurs how to build successful businesses.

I make accounting easy and accurate for Fortune 500 companies.

I work with retailers to help them devise smart floorplans.

From these simple statements, we learn the audience that these people target as well as a benefit of working with them. From that, we can decide if there's a match and a reason to keep talking business.

However you introduce yourself, let your personality shine through. You should be and sound comfortable doing it, which means you'll need to practice and watch what generates the right reaction from others, which should be more questions about what you do. The purpose of your introduction is to open a conversation to explore interest. The formula I have given is a terrific staple, but feel free to get more creative if it suits you.

If you are a personal organizer for example, you could say something like, "I help people find their keys every morning." That would surely get people smiling and asking questions. Then you could explain what you really do.

Do be careful that your introduction doesn't become trite. There are a lot of people saying the same thing such as, "I help people realize their dreams," That doesn't say anything. I've heard something similar come from career consultants, personal trainers, and travel agents. As always, you have to be specific.

Chapter 16

The Power of Questions

Getting to the issues that really matter

People like to talk too much. Salespeople spend too much time talking and not enough time listening. Human resource managers squander sacred interview time by talking more about the company than the job candidate.

People need to talk less and ask more. That's how you learn what you need to know to be successful. That's how you learn what matters to the people you are trying to sway. As a marketer, questions are your greatest allies and your secret weapons. Questions will help you to:

▶ Get focused.

▶ Understand what targets really think about you.

▶ Lead customers to their own resolutions about why they need to buy from you.

▶ Open doors to up-selling and cross-selling.

▶ Keep the conversation going.

▶ Reveal what you need to know to better serve and attract targets.

▶ Help you control where the conversation is going.

▶ Guide your target's train of thinking.

▶ Show interest and build rapport.

▶ Get the customer saying yes.

▶ Listen to the customer and stir positive emotions.

▶ Stand out because no one else is listening.

Questions can help you serve your customers day-to-day. Questions can help you understand the messages that need to be put into the marketplace.

Questions let you know how you're doing and what you need to do differently. Sometimes questions will be the best way to tell your marketing story. As a marketer, you must be skilled in asking productive questions that lead to meaningful answers.

Everyday Marketing Questions

We've talked about many questions already that you need to use every day in your business to be a marketing machine such as:

- ► What is the marketing opportunity here?
- ► What kind of impression are we making here?
- ► Is this impression great, bad, or indifferent?
- ► How can we make a great impression here?
- ► What does the customer want?
- ► What does the customer not want?
- ► What does that mean for the customer?

We also know that all targets come with common questions, such as:

- ► What's in it for me?
- ► What have you done for me lately?
- ► Where are you taking me?

Now let's explore some other ways that questions can help you communicate like a marketer.

Questions to Ask Targets

Use questions to build rapport with targets. Ask them about their days, their businesses, their spouses, their golf games—anything to get them talking and to demonstrate your genuine interest in them as people. Use questions to understand what matters to them. Be direct. Just come out and ask:

- ► What is important to you here?
- ► How can we make things easier for you?
- ► What do you want to see happen?
- ► What would make this work for you?
- ► How can we do a better job for you?

Use Questions to Get Targets Saying Yes

People are too quick to react to a question with an answer. Listen in on five sales presentations, and four will put you to sleep because the leader thinks the meeting is all about him. Your goal as a marketer is always to get the target talking and to get him saying yes. Even if the yes is about something immaterial, you want targets to get in the habit of giving you affirmative answers. Believe me, it works.

You can do this even when a target is asking you a question. Just answer a question with a question whenever it's appropriate. For example, if a target asks, "Does this come in red?" throw it back to him with, "Would you like one in red?" When a target says, "How soon can you do it?" ask him, "When would you like it?"

▪

Start really noticing how often people talk about themselves and how little they ask of others. Start putting the power of questions to work for you and see all of the great marketing morsels you can uncover. The more you ask, the better and easier marketing will be.

Questions for Customer Service

Consider these questions to help you detect areas for improvement in your customer service:

- Do I look at everything from my customer's perspective?
- Do I use the customer's name when I speak to her?
- Are my words polished, or am I always fumbling because I am not confident in what I'm saying?
- Do customers have my business card?
- Do I ever give customers more than they ask for?
- Do I tell customers all that I do for them?
- Do I give more bad news than good news to my customers?
- Do I dedicate quality time and really listen to my customers?
- Do I know more about my customers than their last job, order, purchase, proposal, or estimate?

- Do I tell customers my troubles or share too much behind-the-scenes information?
- Do I blame other people or departments for mistakes and hiccups?
- Do I ask the customer what is important to her?
- Do I take an opportunity to educate my customer anytime I can?
- Do I use the power of questions to market, understand, and further my relationship with customers?
- Do I tell the customer about our products and services on a regular basis?
- Do I offer my customers solutions even when I cannot help them personally?
- Am I apologizing or saying no to customers too often?
- Do I ask for the order?

Chapter 17

Writing a Killer Marketing Letter

Just follow the formula

As an aggressive marketer, you likely will have a lot of letters to write, be they long sales letters or simple cover letters or thank you notes. I have devised a simple, yet effective formula for generating these with clarity, ease, and impact. And you're about to have it.

There is no guesswork when you follow this formula, which contains all of the essential components of a true marketing tool. Just follow the instructions to create a heavy-hitter every time.

The Formula

Strong marketing correspondence contains several key elements including:

- ▶ One central theme
- ▶ A leading statement or headline to get attention
- ▶ Specific details and facts to support your claim
- ▶ Sub-headings if appropriate for the length of the message (even just one full page)
- ▶ Call to action
- ▶ Postscript (The P.S. always gets read, usually first. Never send a letter without one!)
- ▶ Strong, active, positive language
- ▶ Emotion words
- ▶ Appropriate tone
- ▶ Professional appearance
- ▶ Smart packaging
- ▶ Personal touch or add-on to get extra attention (sticky note, hand-written message, or highlighted passage)

Before You Write, Ask

As with all marketing projects, you need to get clear on a few things before you write. Consider each of these questions to gain clarity and confidence on where you need go with each piece:

1. Who is my specific target for this message and what does that mean? What information and style of communication will connect with my target? Do I need to be direct with no fluff and lots of facts? Do I need to paint a visual picture? Is there a particular way my target processes information that I need to take into consideration?

2. What is the central message I must convey in this communication?

3. What do I need my target to know, think, and feel in this communication?

4. What do I want my target to do as a result of this communication?

5. What would my target want to know, think, and feel about the company to decide to choose us?

6. What facts or details need to be included to back up my message?

7. What is the right tone for this piece?

8. What's my headline? How can I get the reader's attention immediately? What message must my target leave with if he gets no other?

9. What do I need to reiterate in my postscript (P.S.) to leave with a heavy punch, motivation to act, or a great sense of urgency?

10. How do I need to set this letter to make it visually appealing and to be consistent with the communication standards established for my company?

11. What personal touches can I add to get attention and make a greater impact?

12. How do I package the communication so it gets opened? (Envelope, strong e-mail subject line, and so on)

With these answers, you are armed and ready to start writing and producing your message.

Simple Formula for an Effective Marketing Letter

Here it is—the simple formula that can make your marketing letters come together in a snap and with great punch. I use it all the time with great success. Review the template and then see the real sample letter that follows.

Dear Mr. Name,

Open with a bang! Get your target's attention immediately with a strong statement or question. Make it bold. Make it bigger.

Add a personal handwritten note here or in the margin to really get attention.

Now that you have their attention, you need to hold it in this critical paragraph. Qualify your opening statement and set the stage for a series of support items to prove your point. You might say something like, "That's why you will find so many good reasons to participate in this program." Now you can easily present the reasons in a simple, clear-cut fashion as standalone subheadings. This will give you a simple structure to follow as you write, and it will make it easy for the reader to glide through the material. It also sets the stage for making your letter scannable with sub-headings. At a glance, your target will be able to catch important marketing points and benefits.

Subheading—Benefit 1

Each sub-heading should be bold to visually stand out. Even choose a different typestyle to add some graphic variety to the piece. In content, each sub-heading should stand alone in making a key point or relating a benefit. Something like "Knowledgeable Staff to Assist You" or "Joining Couldn't Be Any Easier" tells the reader what's in it for him. From there, give the details and facts that support your claim. Keep sentences generally short and tight. Keep on point and speak directly to the reader. Remember to write in terms of "you."

Subheading—Benefit 2

Repeat the same step as before. You need a minimum of three benefits. If you have many items that don't require any real explanation, use a bulleted listing for easy and quick review.

Subheading—Benefit 3

Same thing, one more time.

Now you need a wrap-up paragraph. Here you summarize your core message and benefits. Tie the text back to your opening headline to sew up the letter and leave targets with a strong summary of what you want them to take away with them. Keep it simple and focused.

Call your target to action. Every communication must end with a call to action, and here you should make yours strong and visible. When a target scans your letter, you definitely want the call to action to stand out, so make it bold. Tell your targets exactly what you want them to do next and give them a good reason or incentive to do it right away. Even repeat your contact information to make acting super easy. You may follow up with a pleasantry such as "I look forward to your call," but make your words strong, positive, and action-oriented. Speak as if the deal is a sure-thing, such as, "We look forward to helping you save a lot of money," or "We're ready to get started."

Sincerely,

Use whatever salutation is comfortable to you, but feel free to get a little creative if it suits you and your business. A simple change to something like "enthusiastically" or "confidently" instead of "best regards" adds energy to the letter and makes you stand out.

Name

Title

P.S. Always include a postscript. People always read the P.S., sometimes first. Make the moment count. Motivate them to act again and stress its urgency. Direct them to your Website—and tell them why they need to take the time to go there. Make a special offer. This is valuable real estate so use it well.

Before sending off your letter, add an extra personal touch like a note in the margin in a different color. Attach a sticky note or underline or highlight something in the letter. Anything out of the ordinary will stand out. Of course, put your envelope to work for you. Write a teaser note on the outside. Even choose a larger size or bright color to really get attention (as long as it matches your company's color scheme of course).

A Letter to Baby Sarah

Now let's put the formula into practice, and let's have a little fun with it. In our sample letter, my purpose is to get Baby Sarah to signify that I can continue being her mother. I want her to *know* that I'm a good choice because I will give her the things she needs and wants to be a happy child. I want her to *think* that I am sincere in my wishes to be her mother. I want her to *feel* confident that I'm her best choice for the role, and that I can deliver on my promises.

Now, thinking about what's important to Baby Sarah, I know she wants good food, prompt diaper changes, and lots of love. That's really all she cares about, so that's what I as the marketer need to address in my letter.

So here goes...

Dear Sarah,

You are a lucky girl!

I love being your mother and I am willing to do whatever it takes to care for you and make you feel happy and loved, and to make you proud to have me. When you choose me as your mother, you're sure to enjoy many wonderful benefits.

Great Food and Snacks

My pantry is always stocked with you in mind. Your favorite snacks such as dehydrated corn, bananas, and a variety of cereals are ready and waiting for you anytime you need them. Plus, you'll find mint chocolate chip ice cream a permanent fixture in my freezer, so you always have something to soothe those sore gums.

Prompt Diaper Changes

I know that getting your diaper changed quickly is important to you. That's why I have fully equipped all rooms of the house. When a need is detected, I can clean you up immediately.

Endless Hugs and Kisses

You won't believe all of the hugs and kisses that you are going to get for the rest of your life. When you wake up, when you go to bed, and a hundred times in between, you'll be swarmed with love.

I certainly feel very lucky to be your mother and I am confident that you will continue to find me the perfect person to feed, change, and love you forever. **If you agree, simply give me a quick squeeze of my nose, and it will be official.**

I look forward to being the best mother you could ever wish for.

Lovingly,

Mom

P.S. I will also buy you lots of toys and send you to a good college. Go ahead, give my nose a good squeeze right now!

That may be a silly example, but marketing applies everywhere. The concern here is formula, and this letter fits the form perfectly. Notice the simple headline—You're a lucky girl! As the reader, wouldn't you want to know why you're lucky?

The sub-headings relay benefits and they prove the point made in the headline. This letter is perfectly clear in telling the target what's in it for her. Notice also that the headline theme comes back around at the end of the letter to tightly sew up and reiterate the concept. Of course there is a clear call to action in this piece as well as a postscript that gives another benefit and another push to act immediately.

As you scan through the letter, you'll find lots of "you's" and many emotion words like love, lucky, care, proud, favorite, confident, important, and enthusiastically. The tone is upbeat and strong from start to finish. If you were Sarah, wouldn't you keep me as your mother?

After You Write

After you have drafted and given your marketing letter at least two reviews to kick up your language, use these questions to assess your work:

1. Is it easy to get your eyes into? Are paragraphs short? Is there enough white space to make it visually comfortable and easy to read?

2. Is it scannable? Do key points jump off the page and collectively tell a complete story? Can the reader "get" your message by just glancing at the letter and all of the parts that stand out?

3. Does it capture the reader's attention immediately?

4. Do I speak to the reader directly by using "you" often? Is the message more about my reader than about me/us?

5. Do I tell the reader what's in it for him? Are the benefits clear?

6. Does it convey or stir the right emotions?

7. Does it reflect the personality of our company?

8. Do I sound confident in my words, claims, products, and services?

9. Do I use strong, active, positive words?

10. Have I sifted out all of the weak words and expressions like *hope* and *hesitate to call?*

11. Does it flow easily and make my point effectively? Can the reader understand my message in just one read?

12. Is it accurate in grammar, spelling, and punctuation?

13. Do I vary the length and style of my sentences for interest and variety? Does it flow well when I read it out loud?

14. Does it close with a strong call to action? Is it very clear what I want the reader to do next? Have I given her motivation to do that?

15. Is the P.S. strong? Does it motivate the reader to act? Does it leave them with a great last impression?

16. If the target just read the opening sentence, sub-headings, call to action, and postscript, would he understand the central message and be motivated to act?

17. Is it set in a font size and style that is easy to read, visually appealing, and consistent with the personality of the company?

18. Did I proofread it at least two times? Do I need someone else to read it before it goes out?

19. Have I added a personal touch for effectiveness if needed, appropriate, or feasible?

20. Do I need to include a business card, support information, fun item, or anything else that would make the communication more memorable and effective?

21. Do I need to do anything with the envelope or packaging to make sure my message gets read? (Professional label. Message on the outside. Something bulky in the package.)

22. What would I think—and do—if I received this package?

Something to Think About

▶ What questions do you need to start asking right now?

▶ What do you need to do or focus on to make your marketing communications more effective?

▶ What are you currently using that needs to be re-done?

TIPS 63–89
of How to Put Your Marketing Into Action

63. **Make phone "hold time" productive.** You have your caller's attention so put it to good use. Pipe in a professional, well-written message about your company and your offerings while they hold. Turn it into a radio format where you share quick tips. Or, do something really different like feature comedy to give callers something great to talk about. However you use it, hold time is a big marketing opportunity. Make it work for you.

64. **Add marketing punch to your voice mail.** Dump the robotic tone and the standard, boring message. Get creative. Make "going to voice mail" a pleasant experience with a message that is interesting, entertaining, and educational for your callers. Change it up frequently to give callers something new.

65. **Be prepared for objections.** You're sure to get objections, so you need to be rehearsed and ready for them. Start by listing every possible objection a customer might give you. Construct a clear answer for each of them in writing. Practice them until you sound natural and confident in your delivery. Then, when you get an objection, you can say, "That's exactly the reason you need me, and here's why."

66. **Business is always fantastic unless everyone knows it isn't.** Complaining to customers about a slump in business certainly won't instill confidence, though non-marketers do it all the time. Keep your comments positive or at least vague, but never negative.

67. **Give people warnings beforehand.** When something might or could go wrong, tell people upfront. That makes you smart. Do it afterward and it sounds like an excuse.

68. **Are you apologizing too much?** "Sorry for the wait." "I apologize for that error." "I'm sorry you had that problem." When an apology is necessary, be quick to give it, but pay attention if you're serving up apologies too frequently. If so, that's your red flag that something needs adjusting. So what are you apologizing for, and how often? Identify areas that need immediate attention.

69. **Give customers the confidence of confirmation.** People want to know that things are happening timely or as promised. (They certainly want to know if things have fallen off course.) Give customers the security of a simple phone call, e-mail, or postcard to let them know that the appointment is still scheduled, the order has been shipped, or things are working as they should be, or not. Even if it's just to acknowledge receipt of one's call, fax, or e-mail, don't leave people hanging. Give them the closure of confirmation.

70. **Never utter, "May I ask who's calling?"** It's a common question, but it's interrogatory and just not polite for people whom you're begging to call you. Instead ask, "May I *tell* him/her who's calling?" It's more active and has a more cordial ring to it.

71. **Keep your troubles to yourself.** Boss trouble, boyfriend trouble, money trouble, too-much-work trouble—that is all too much information for your customers. Staff share personal woes all the time and it's both unprofessional and unwise. Frankly, customers don't care about your personal issues and, by telling them, you only shake their confidence in your ability to focus and serve them well. If you need to lament your troubles, go where you are the customer so the company has to listen to you. Otherwise, keep all comments upbeat, positive, or strictly about the customer.

72. **What drives you crazy on the phone?** Getting passed around? Being interrogated by a receptionist? Too many menus to navigate through? Chances are your customers hate those things as well, and we all know that it's the little things that can bother us most. List at least three of your own telephone pet peeves. Are you certain that your company is not guilty of the same things—ever? How about yourself? Train everyone who ever answers a telephone in your business. Mystery call your own company. Keep close attention on what's happening on your telephone.

73. **Act like you know them, even if you don't.** A sure way to make customers (or anyone) feel special is to use their name in a pleasant tone. Whether it's over the phone, in a sales call, or in a networking meeting, show excitement when you first meet anybody. Be cordial, excited, and sincere. Greet them as if you already know them, and they'll love you right from the start.

74. **Thank them even when you don't get the business.** Marketing never ends, and that applies even when you lose a bid, contract, or customer. Position yourself well for the next opportunity by leaving targets with a great impression. Show your good character by thanking them for their business or for the opportunity to compete for it. Send a cake or other gift to really get their attention. Of course, touch base with them periodically and keep them in your marketing program. Who knows what opportunities tomorrow may bring?

75. **Pick up the phone.** In a world where everyone depends on electronic communications, the personal contact of a phone call will certainly get you noticed. Plus, it will move business forward. Don't let important business sit while you wait for an e-mail. Just because you clicked to send a message doesn't mean it was received. It's easy to hide behind e-mail, but sometimes it's not the best thing for your business. Keep things moving by picking up the phone when you need to.

76. **Could a stranger understand what you do just by looking at you?** Is what you do clear in your signage, printed materials, Website, front door, reception area, packaging, and everything else that is you or that represents you? Do you need a tag line to accompany your logo to explain what you do? Who you are and what you do should always be evident at face value. If someone has to ask, then adjustments need to be made. Take a look around. Are you hiding your true identity?

77. **Start strong, finish strong on every page of your Website.** Lead every page of your Website with a strong headline and close with a strong call to action. Start by telling them what you can do for them. Finish by telling them what you want them to do next to get it. In the middle, make your pages scannable and your message easy to discern. Don't make them have to think or dig too hard. Go for attention, brevity, and clarity. Be simple, clear, and direct.

78. **Stay up late for the infomercials.** (Just hold on tight to your credit cards.) It's no secret that the infomercial is there to make you buy, yet still you stop to watch for a while and maybe even purchase another piece of exercise equipment. Why? What is it about the infomercial that draws us in, holds us there, and makes us want to reach for our credit card? It's a proven formula and it can work for your business, too. Bold statements. Live testimonials. Lots of repetition. Easy purchasing. Strong call to action with an incentive to act now. It's all there. Is it all there in your marketing materials?

79. **Love junk mail.** Consider junk mail as free research. Pay attention to your mailbox and your e-mail box every day. What catches your attention and why? What makes you want to act and why? What makes you immediately head to the trashcan and why? However it impacts you is a good indicator of how it might impact your target audience. Hang on to junk mail. Keep what you love. Keep what you hate. Maintain a file to refer to when you're developing your own mail pieces.

80. **Leave "homemade" to cookies and holiday ornaments.** Take a look at what's going out of your company. Are all brochures, forms, flyers, and other materials representing you well? Are they consistent with the standards you set for your company's image and identity? Homemade communications are acceptable as long as they don't look homemade. Take a look at your materials. Is every piece making the impression you want to make? Be honest.

81. **Show "proof of performance."** The case study is always an effective marketing tool because it demonstrates that you really do what your marketing says you do. Tell the world when you do a good job. Present real-life stories of how you helped customers solve problems and include customer comments for extra credibility. Develop a series of stories and make flyers for each. Put them on your Website, in a newsletter, in your brochure, everywhere. What stories will help you sell? Take action today toward getting at least one "proof of performance" story done and working for you.

82. **Romance the media.** Publicity is free and powerful marketing, so you definitely want to make getting it one of your marketing goals. You get news coverage by offering something newsworthy to the media—information that is relevant and timely. Learn how to write good press releases and send

them regularly. Make contact with media reps to introduce yourself and offer your expertise when they need a sound byte or quote for an article. Send them tips and other resource information that can serve their readers. And always, always meet their deadlines. The more dependable and accessible you are, the more often they'll look your way. Look to media offline and online.

83. **What is the personality of your marketing materials?** How would a prospect or outsider describe your company by the way your marketing materials look, read, and sound? Do your materials reflect your company or someone else? Is there a disconnect between what people see and what they get? What needs to be emphasized, eliminated, or revised in your marketing communications to adequately reflect who you really are?

84. **Make sure your copywriter adopts your voice.** There is no required tone for your marketing materials, except that it should appeal to your target market and accurately reflect the personality of your company. Even if you hire someone to form the words, your marketing text should sound like it's coming from you. If you're a casual company, the text should be casual. If you're a formal company, the text should be more formal. Make sure your marketing copy reflects your voice, not your copywriter's.

85. **Watch your words.** Some words should never be uttered to customers, not if you want to be perceived as courteous and professional. The word "furthermore" always carries a negative undertone, as well as a formality as if you're giving a legal dictate. Customers should never be rudely told to do anything "ASAP." And, anytime you tell a customer that they can't do something, you're taking a big risk. Watch and listen to how your company speaks to customers. Poor word choices can be costly.

86. **Ask for the order.** Your target audience has your money and they are willing to give it you, but you have to ask them. I have heard CEOs complain about salespeople who begged for a meeting, got it, and then never asked for the business. They felt slighted and that their time was wasted. Always ask for the order. Remember, you don't get it if you don't ask.

87. **Have good news to report regularly.** Keep prospects and customers attuned by sharing news with them regularly. It can definitely be challenging to constantly have something new or exciting to tell, but don't overlook

events like new employees, a job well done for a customer, technology upgrades, an anniversary, or a record month or quarter. You need reasons to talk to your customers on a regular basis, so be a news hound, constantly sniffing out stories to share. This is part of telling them what you've done for them lately.

88. **Get everyone saying "yes."** Get prospects and customers in the habit of saying "yes" to you by constructing questions that present "yes opportunities" regularly be it in a formal presentation or simple conversation. Ask, "Can you relate to that?" or "Does that ever happen to you?" or "Can you see how this could work in your organization?" or "Does that make good sense for you?" This will get them primed and ready to say "yes" when you pop the big question: "Are you ready to buy?"

89. **Make a great last impression.** Making a good first impression keeps the exchange going, but it's the last impression that sticks. It's like telling a joke. You have to get the ending right. So what's your punch line? What message do you leave them with? What's the emotion or energy level you finish on? These questions must be asked and answered in everything you do—every brochure, Web page, proposal, demonstration, service situation, phone call, everything. Don't let the ending fizzle. Leave with an exclamation mark. Have a great punch line. Go out with a bang!

Keeping Marketing in Motion

Marketing must be constant in thought and constant in action.

Chapter 18

Avoiding Common Marketing Mistakes

Preventing backward steps

Before you launch into your new marketing regimen, let's explore some common mistakes that can impede your marketing success. These infractions are committed by marketing newbies and seasoned professionals alike, so don't be ashamed if you're guilty. Just remind yourself that you're thinking like a marketer now.

Hold your focus and avoid these mistakes at all costs.

Mistake 1: Underestimate your real impact on customers.

To remain effective in your marketing, your company must remain clear, passionate, and genuinely excited about the value you bring to the marketplace. And, most importantly, you must know exactly what that is. You may need to sharpen the picture every now and then to keep everyone focused on the real impact they have in customers' lives and businesses.

Mistake 2: Focus too much on running your business than building your business.

This should be a minimal risk now that you know how to make marketing practical and routine. Still, it is easy to get buried in the trivia and tedium of busyness. You will need to dedicate yourself to maintaining balance between working on the business and working in it. Right now ask yourself how much time you personally dedicated to your marketing in the last 60 days. Rate your current marketing aggressiveness on a scale of 1-5. Are you happy with those answers? Will they help you achieve your business goals? Your personal goals? What is your ideal level of marketing aggressiveness and how can you make that happen? What do you need to do more of? Less of? What do you need to stop doing? Start doing? If you haven't already begun to implement what you've learned in this text, start today. You're losing opportunities. Get your marketing machine moving!

Mistake 3: Make marketing so complicated that it doesn't get done.

Now you know how to streamline and simplify your marketing. You have real tools and methods to use and sound principles to guide you. Beware, however, that the marketing-minded have a natural tendency to over-reach, over-analyze, and over-complicate. Remind yourself that you do not have to do everything at once, just something. Your goal is always well done, not perfect. If you do get stuck in "overwhelm mode," just pick one thing you can finish and do it. Remember, nothing counts until you cross the finish line, and it's important that you act swiftly. Opportunities are lost every day because people move too slowly while they pick, mull, and obsess. Ask the right questions to help you make smart, quick decisions. Sometimes seconds count, and no doubt the dynamics change as time ticks by. Even a returned telephone call takes on a different tone when it's made a day after the original call. Be a warrior for simplicity. If it's not simple, you won't do it, and marketing is not an option.

Mistake 4: Hesitate to spend money.

I understand that money has to be present before it can be spent, but marketing must be a priority in your budgeting. You will need to spend money to make money. People often ask me how much is the right amount to spend. It's hard to say because every company's circumstances are different and a flat percentage can be terribly skewed when comparing companies at opposite ends of the sales spectrum. Here's one rule: If you're spending more money on office supplies, then you need to check your priorities and amp up your marketing investment.

If forced to give a number, I, like most experts, will say about 10 percent of your total budget, but even that makes me nervous. I know companies who spend 5 percent and get great returns and others who spend 20 percent and get little results. I think it's a moot point anyway because most small and mid-size companies aren't spending nearly enough, or they're not spending wisely. Sure, you need to watch your budget, but you cannot overlook the critical importance of your marketing. It must happen. Do a good job of tracking results and you'll have the data you need to make confident choices as to where you put your money.

In truth, there's a different issue at play. The real reason for hesitation is often not the lack of money, but rather the lack of certainty. If you were guaranteed that spending every penny you had would give you more in return, you would do it. Because you will likely never have that assurance, you're going to have to take some chances. Just make them calculated.

Mistake 5: Do production work you aren't qualified to do.

This often follows suit with hesitating to spend money. Just because you can do something doesn't mean you should. If you are not a great copywriter, get someone else to write your marketing materials. If you're not a professional designer, hire someone who is. Your image and business future are at stake. Everything you use to represent you must tell an accurate story about you, and if your communications are looking amateur, then you're not sending the right message. Accept that sometimes you will need to pay for professional assistance. It doesn't have to be expensive, though. Hire talented high school and college students for drastically reduced rates. Hire a designer to develop a graphic template that you can repurpose as you go.

Making great impressions often takes a team. Don't let pride, money, or your love for tinkering on the computer jeopardize your impressions in the marketplace. Everything is marketing, and everything can help or hurt you. Spend your time and energies where you excel. Vend out the rest.

Mistake 6: Try to be too professional.

Sometimes people take professional to the point of being stiff and stilted. Yes, your materials need to look professionally produced, and you need to uphold high standards in serving your customers. That does not mean, however, that you cannot let your hair down a bit. In the end, you're doing business with people, and people want to know that you're real. Be personal. Put a face on your company. Introduce customers to the people who are serving them. In all of your communications, talk to targets as if they were sitting right in front of you. Be silly if you need to be silly to make your products and services more appealing. Be professional, but most of all, be personal.

Mistake 7: Fly by the seat of your pants.

You cannot make great things happen if you are running around with your pants on fire and leaving everything to chance. Even luck is not that lucky. You must operate from a position of knowledge, attention, and strategy. Be flexible and nimble, but work with direction. It takes a lot of work to make coincidence happen. Develop your plan and work your plan. This is your business. This is your life.

Mistake 8: Don't make marketing routine.

Haphazard marketing is never going to give you the results you want or build the marketing momentum you need. It will keep you in a state of frustration and lackluster results. Now that you are enlightened and equipped to think, act, and communicate like a marketer, you can avoid this fate—as long as you remain committed to the cause. Constantly ask the powerful question, *What is the marketing opportunity here?* Apply everything you've learned to integrate marketing into every aspect of your business. Keep marketing constant in thought and constant in action.

Mistake 9: Don't maintain a reliable database.

Your database is your pot of gold, and it must remain well polished and well stirred. The greatest of marketing efforts will fail if the list is poor. Therefore, you must have a solid, growing, and well-maintained database and someone to drive it. By the way, your Accounts Receivable list is not your marketing database! You'll need separate and extractable databases for each of your target audiences. This is not negotiable. The quality of your database largely determines the quality of your results.

Mistake 10: Have scatter-brained messages and efforts.

All of that change and variety will just exhaust you and your resources, and worse, nothing will stick. Now you well know that consistency is the golden ticket to everything you do in your marketing. Get a good message out there and leave it alone.

Mistake 11: Talk only about yourself.

Now that you've learned how to talk like a marketer, I'm sure you'll be much smarter on this front. Still, I will caution you to keep tight watch on every communication that comes out of your business. Make sure "you" is more popular than "we."

Mistake 12: Data dump.

Every day I see people unload their entire marketing toolkit in one Big Bang effect. They give away everything they have—their entire story, all of their materials and fun gadgets—right out of the shoot. With it taking an average minimum of seven to nine touches to hit a target's radar, you can understand why it's important to spread things out a bit. Let your marketing build.

Save something for the next contact. In marketing to the masses, you'll be better served by a steady trickle than a tidal wave.

Mistake 13: Try to reach too many targets too little.

It's natural to want to reach everyone who could buy your products and services, but it's not always practical. If the cost is too great to reach everyone, then scale back your list or scope. It's better to reach fewer targets more often than more targets less frequently. Let me say that again. It's better to reach fewer people more often than more people less often. If you're running print ads, reduce the size of the ad if necessary to allow for a longer run time. When you're watching the money, go deep, not wide.

Mistake 14: Miss marketing opportunities inherent in the day-to-day running of your business.

This should be a non-issue for you by now, though it will take some practice to train your eyes to notice what you once neglected. Just consider it a fun scavenger hunt to find more and more opportunities to make great impressions and market your business.

Standing in line at Starbucks, I became frustrated as a customer when I realized they were un-stocked with one of my favorite items. As a marketer, however, I enjoyed a light chuckle when I saw the printing that took its place. The sign read, *Bad news: out today. Good news: more in the morning.* That's a small marketing opportunity, but they took advantage of it, and I did return the next morning to get my yogurt cup. Marketing opportunities are everywhere. The more you look, the more you find.

Mistake 15: Don't know what to do, so you do nothing at all.

It's easy to become overwhelmed with all of those big ideas swirling in your brain and all of those possibilities jumping out at you, but don't allow yourself to become overwhelmed to the point of being paralyzed. When you feel yourself getting tense, just take a deep breath and consider where you can make the most impact the fastest. Finish something you've been working on. Call a customer. Write a letter. Do one thing that you can complete quickly. Closure is a beautiful thing and it can do wonders for regaining focus and circulation. If you really don't know what to do in your marketing, listen to your instincts. They will tell you where your efforts are best served. Better yet, you can consult your detailed and carefully devised Marketing Plan. If you're at a total loss, start with your current customers or just pick up the phone. Those moves are always safe and productive. The most important thing is that you just do something.

Mistake 16: Give up too soon on a marketing initiative.

You must give marketing time to work. Sure, we all enjoy instant gratification, and it's easy to get impatient when new business doesn't come flooding in. Your diligence and persistence will be highly rewarded as you build and maintain marketing momentum. Success in marketing comes from the culmination of lots of little things happening all the time. Do your homework and then stay the course. Be patient. Be confident. Just keep stirring!

Something to Think About

▶ So, what marketing mistake is hurting you most right now and how can you correct it?

▶ How can you prevent your company from becoming a victim of any of these common mistakes?

Chapter 19

Maintaining a Marketing Mindset

How to keep marketing top of mind, all the time

You know well by now that, to be a marketing machine, everyone in your business must be thinking, acting, and communicating like a marketer every day. That means you need everyone operating in the right, and same, frame of mind.

I have a few final suggestions to help you maintain a marketing mindset throughout your company. Do not pick and choose. Do all of them. They will not only make you a better marketer, they'll make you a better business. Of course being a better business gives you a better story to market. A better story means customers love you more. More love means great word-of-mouth. That, in turn, drives in more customers. And around and around you go in your giant pot of fabulous marketing gumbo.

1. Get your entire team involved in developing your marketing plan.

Everyone needs to be heard and everyone has ideas to be considered. Your marketing program may fall solely to you or a handful of others, but you need the value of all perspectives, especially those in the trenches and closest to the customer. Ask questions and get your team talking, brainstorming, and masterminding. You'll obtain meaningful input to help your business and boost morale in the process. Even if you do conduct customer research, you still want to tap into the goldmine of information that's running about your company every moment. Your employees have information you need to know, but you'll have to ask to obtain it.

2. Share your marketing plan with your entire company.

Once you have your official marketing plan pulled together, throw it to your team for feedback and buy-in. Everything you do in your marketing will come back around to your team one way or another. They'll have to answer questions about promotions, handle the newly-generated business, watch you cry when things take longer than expected, and continue to form opinions about whether or not you're a company with growth potential. Your team can't help you market the business if they don't know what's going on, so keep them informed.

3. Tell your staff what's in it for them.

Your employees are your internal customers when it comes to implementing your marketing strategy day-to-day. Tell them why it's in their best interest to make great impressions, reinforce the company's image and identity, and overall make customers love you. Like all targets, you'll need to stir their awareness, emotions, and mindfulness to achieve conviction and support for the cause. Like all targets, they'll want to know what's in it for them. Put your new marketing skills to work to tell them what's in it for them to be great marketers in what they do. The answer must be something greater than just "keep your job" (though in a tough economy that might be enough). To breed genuine enthusiasm for your company and your marketing mission, make it worthwhile for employees to go the extra marketing mile. Catch them doing good and applaud them publicly. Reward them with attention, gifts, words of affirmation, quality time, and acts of service. Help employees see the fruits of their marketing efforts, no matter how small or seemingly insignificant they are.

4. Demonstrate that marketing is a top priority for the company.

If marketing isn't evidently important to you, it won't be for your team. Make it a regular topic of conversation. Hold "marketing moments" in staff meetings to discuss recent events, new customers, tips, ideas, and the next steps in your marketing plan. Make it interactive.

In addition, don't allow the "I'm waiting for" syndrome to attack your culture. It's easy for marketing to become stagnant while a person or department blaims another for delaying a project. Someone always seems to be waiting for something. Don't allow this disease to creep in. Likewise, don't allow perfection to overtake you. Something imperfect working for you is better than almost perfect sitting on your desk. Sure, sometimes you will have legitimate reasons to delay, alter, or even postpone marketing efforts, but make sure they are absolutely necessary when you do. Create a sense of urgency and hold people to task. You have too much to lose by being lax, and once marketing starts slipping down the priority pole, it's hard to pull it back.

5. Define the marketing role of every employee.

As we've covered in Phase 1, every employee, no matter their duty, serves a valuable function in the overall marketability and marketing impact of your business. Establish a 30-day deadline to outline on paper the marketing role of each team member. Meet with each person individually to discuss his or her role and the expectations of the company. Help everyone understand what marketing means for them in their respective day-to-day duties. Don't just tell them what to do, tell them *how* to do it.

6. Train every employee on the basics of marketing.

If everyone is a marketer, shouldn't they be trained on how to be a good one? Teach your team the principles covered in this book. Help them understand the power of their words and how to use them to promote the company and improve customer relationships with both customers and their coworkers. Help them understand the impact of their actions and attitudes. Empowering your staff with these skills, even on a rudimentary level, will make you a stronger organization internally and for your customers. Make marketing training a constant component in your marketing strategy. Smart employees make smart companies.

7. Get your team excited about marketing.

Marketing should be some of the most enjoyable work you do. The more excited you are, the more excited your team will be. To rile everybody up, post fun motivations throughout the workplace. Throw parties to celebrate successes large and small such as new inquiries, new customers, sales, profits, great ideas, and seized opportunities. Discuss plans, goals, and improvements. Get everyone involved with contests, brainstorming sessions, and special projects. Host a "question of the week" to get the team thinking together. Create company-wide events with customers and take field trips to see good marketing in other companies. Be creative and have fun. Everybody wants to work for an active, growing company, so build pride by getting everyone involved in your marketing.

8. Divide and conquer.

If your business consists of two or more people, someone must be assigned marketing director. Someone must be the caretaker and driver of the program, making sure marketing is always on the priority and to-do list. If you are an independent entrepreneur, you get to wear the prestigious hat, though you may want to recruit some outside help for strategy planning and administrative assistance. If your company consists of at least 10 or more people, you will be well served to form a marketing committee with representatives from each of the four core areas of the company (operations, accounting, human resources, and business development). They might not be able to help you write copy for your next marketing letter, but they will be helpful in telling you what it needs to say. Marketing is too vast to tackle alone if you are to do it well. Build your support teams to help you make marketing happen.

9. Post marketing motivators and reminders around the workplace.

The adage "out of sight, out of mind" rings loud and true. To keep your team mindful of marketing, you may need some visual assistance. I suggest a dedicated marketing bulletin board. Post samples of marketing communications so everyone can see what's happening and what messages you're sending to the marketplace. Hang motivations, comments from customers, and reminders to keep your marketing on track, such as:

How can we make a great impression here?

What is the marketing opportunity here?

Get out of the gray.

Just start.

Stir awareness, emotions, mindfulness, conviction, and word-of-mouth.

Our marketing is doing good work even if we can't see it yet.

What can we finish today?

10. Make your team accountable for upholding your marketing standards and systems.

It's a leader's death sentence to direct staff to behave a certain way and then not hold them to it. If you are serious about being a marketing machine, you must hold yourself and everyone accountable for making great impressions, following through on plans, and meeting deadlines. Reward publicly those who do and reprimand privately those who don't.

11. Hold faith in your marketing.

Remember, marketing takes commitment and usually more time than you'd like. The more you do it, the more momentum you'll build and the faster you'll see results. Remember also that you can never know all the good your marketing is doing behind the scenes. Remind yourself and your team of this often. Just because you're not getting a flood of calls or new business immediately doesn't mean your efforts aren't working. Remember the seven-to-nine rule to even hit your target's radar. Even if targets are clicking off your e-mails, throwing away your direct mail, or not taking your calls, the point is that you've made a contact with them, and that definitely counts. You're building awareness and, with repetition, you'll earn mindfulness so they will think of you when they want or need what you offer. As long as you continue to take conscious, deliberate steps to stir the pot and keep your marketing in motion, you will see results. Why would you want to chance anything less? Hold faith and keep stirring!

Chapter 20

Stirring the Pot When You're the Pot

Keeping yourself committed

Sometimes our most challenging target audience, or "pot," is ourselves. I see it all the time with my customers. An owner will say that he wants to make things happen in his business, but when it really comes down to it, he's not comfortable stirring things up. He is sincere in his wishes, but when it's time to make a decision or take action, he's nervous, reserved, even paralyzed. He will spout logical reasons why derailment of his marketing plan is justified, but they won't be the real ones. I'll watch him fidget as he grumbles about budgets and busy work schedules, but I'll know. I've seen it a hundred times. Hey, I'm a business owner myself. I share the same worries and concerns and uncertainties. But I know that nothing ventured is nothing gained, and I know I can't attract customers and build my business unless I take conscious, deliberate action to do it.

There's no better chance worth taking and no work more important than marketing your company. You must do it and you must push yourself if you're the one getting in the way of progress. It all comes down to commitment. Are you really serious about making and building a great business?

If you ever find yourself being hesitant, reserved, and unable to make a move or take a risk, be honest about why you're there. Then pull out your big spoon and get to stirring—on yourself.

Stir Awareness

Keep what you're working for in mind. Post your marketing goals where you can look at them every day. Visualize how great it will be to have those sales, customers, and advancements in your business. Envision the fun of working when business is flowing. See that big number at the bottom of your P&L statement. Picture finally buying that equipment you've been wanting.

The more real the image of success, the more excited and anxious you'll be to focus on your marketing. Another helpful technique is to declare affirmations. I read once that Bill Gates regularly walked down the Microsoft halls quietly chanting to himself, "I am making money. I am making money." Try these for yourself:

▶ I am a marketing machine.

▶ Marketing is the path to my goals.

▶ Marketing is fun and easy.

▶ I am a smart and confident marketer.

▶ I am making a great present and future for my business when I market.

▶ The more I do, the more that comes back to me.

▶ I am making an impact in everything I do whether I see it or not.

▶ Marketing can help me be wildly successful faster.

As with all marketing, you'll need repetition to make them work. Say them several times a day. Writing them down is even more powerful.

Another important technique is starting each day with the question, *What do I need to do to stir the pot in my business today?* List at least three things. If you have worked through your Marketing Detail, you will know exactly what to do at all times to make your goals happen. Push yourself to make that call, send that e-mail, and connect with that person who has been "on your list." You'll be so pleased with yourself and wonder what took you so long. The more you do, the easier it gets, and the sweet thrill of completion will take over. Your priorities will shift, and suddenly, finally, you will put yourself and your business first.

Stir Emotion

How will you feel when you achieve your marketing goals? Excited, successful, comfortable, secure? Play it out in your mind. Hear customers and associates compliment you. See the excitement when you announce your record monthly sales. Go ahead, write down that number and admire it for a moment. Actor Jim Carey tells a terrific story about how, long before the public knew his name, he wrote himself a check for $10,000,000 to simulate his fee for a blockbuster hit movie. He carried it in his wallet and looked at it every day. Make your goals as real as you can so you can stir your own emotions. One fun trick is to write down the headlines that describe your success, such as:

My Company Tops Forbes' List for Up-and-Coming Companies

My Company Sets Sales Record for the Industry and Gets to Buy New Building and Shiny New Equipment

Company Owner Meets All Obligations with Financial Ease

Company Owner Basks in Profits While Vacationing in the Bahamas

Consider the contrary also. What headlines could you write if you leave marketing on the bottom of the priority pole? If you don't take advantage of the marketing opportunities right under your nose? If you don't keep marketing constant in thought and constant in action? If you stop stirring the pot? Keep yourself committed to your marketing cause by stirring your own emotions.

Stir Mindfulness

Do whatever it takes to keep marketing at the top of your mind. Follow the steps you learned in the last chapter. Put a simple, red plastic spoon in your pencil cup to be a visual reminder to stir the pot and keep your marketing moving.

If you do at least half of what you've learned here, marketing will be on your radar at all times. The program will pull you until marketing becomes second-nature and a comfortable part of your operation. You just have to get the wheels moving. Pledge to do something today to help you keep marketing constant in thought so it can be constant in action.

Stir Conviction

Just as you must constantly tell your customers what's in it for them and what you've done for them lately, you may need a little reminding yourself.

Refresh your thinking on the impact and value you have on your company, staff, customers, marketplace, industry, and others. What would happen if you went out of business tomorrow? Who would be affected and how? None of us live or work in a vacuum. Everything we do has an impact. Just like the "butterfly effect," every move you make alters the dynamics around you, so keep yourself attuned and ingrained in what's happening in your business every day. Hang out in the lobby or the Customer Service Department for a while. Ask how new inquiries heard of you or found you online. Thank new customers personally for their business and gather their impressions.

To maintain perspective, you may have to pull yourself away from the tax bill, lease agreement, and bank statement to get in touch with what's really happening in your business. Whatever it takes, do it. There is indeed much in it for you to keep your marketing moving.

Stir Word-of-Mouth

As with customers, when you pass through the previous four stages, you become excited about marketing and what you're doing in your business. Your emotions will become contagious. Others will share in your enthusiasm. People will want to help you. They will make referrals for you. They will introduce you to people you need to know. The viral effect will take off, and success will come faster and more easily. You'll reap the benefits of all that hard work along the way.

With the demands and pressures of any small or mid-size enterprise, it's reasonable to expect your marketing motivation to wane or be overshadowed at times. In fact, it's almost certain to happen. The solution is to create an environment that keeps you motivated just as you work to motivate your own targets. Stirring the pot will work for your targets, and it will work for you.

Chapter 21

Final Call to Action

Just keep stirring

Before I let you loose to stand out, stir the pot, and turn your company into a marketing machine, let me leave you with a few critical reminders.

Starting is the hardest part. Philospher Plato said, "The beginning is the most important part of the work." A Greek proverb states, "A job well begun is half done." It's time for you to start putting your marketing into action. Go back through the phases and take each step one by one. Don't worry about the whole just yet. Take the process piece by piece and, almost like magic, all of the parts will come together.

If you are a procrastinator, you may want to try a technique that has worked wonders for me. I give myself permission to do something for just five minutes. I can do anything for five minutes. After that, I have full right and authority to quit without guilt or recourse.

Oddly, however, I never stop at just five minutes because, once I start, I realize the task wasn't nearly as awful as I had imagined it to be. I start to figure things out, get on a roll, and actually see the possibility of completion. Sometimes I even finish the task within those five minutes, which means all of those hours, weeks, and months of worry and procrastination were sinfully wasted.

The more you plunge yourself into the details of your marketing, the easier it gets. The more you do, the more you will want to do. All you have to do is start. Give yourself just five minutes and watch what happens.

Before you know it, marketing won't be such a big deal. After you put these principles and techniques into practice for a while, you won't even recognize them as extra steps. Marketing will be as natural and common as every other standard business function. You will reach the state described by Richard Koch in *Living the 80/20 Way,* where doing it will be easier than not doing it. When that happens, you will have definitely arrived as a marketing machine.

You can never know the good work your marketing is doing behind the scenes. It is extremely important to remind yourself of this often. When you're frustrated, working hard, spending money, and unsure if any of it is doing any good, take a deep breath. Maybe you do need to alter your plan. Maybe there's something that could work better for you. Or, maybe you just need to be patient. I'll assume the risk of sounding trite as I remind you about the power of the seed. When a seed sits in the ground, it needs time to germinate before you have any visible or tangible indication that it's doing anything. Too bad marketing couldn't be more like an expectant mother whose belly gives us all a visible reading of her progress. I'm afraid we're going to have to stick with the planting analogy. But look around. There are plants and trees everywhere that began the same way our marketing begins—as a speck with hopes of becoming something mighty. Meanwhile, under the dirt and the rain and the sunlight, something meaningful is always happening.

So let's turn the tables once again and put you in the customer seat. Your name is in thousands of people's databases and target lists all over the country or the world. Thousands of individuals, companies, and organizations are scratching their heads and spending their dollars every day trying to lure you to their Website or store. They are working fiercely to get you to call now and order quickly while supplies last. They are giving you reason after reason to choose them and sign on the line which is dotted. And yet, there you are, buzzing around your daily life working on a business, taking care of family, and trying to maintain a couple hobbies and a social life. You're not calling, clicking, signing, or stopping by, and they are becoming exasperated with you and the process. They want to give up and stop wasting their money on you. You're not biting fast enough and they're getting impatient.

But there's something they don't understand. They don't know that you've looked at their messages and considered giving them a try. They don't know you filed away their ad because you've been thinking about painting the fence or getting your teeth cleaned. They don't know that you earmarked their product as the perfect gift for your daughter's birthday. They don't know that your contract is about to expire with your current vendor and that you'll be shopping around soon.

Progress comes in many forms, and just because you can't see it doesn't mean it's not happening. Things change and evolve. People who are not targets for you today could be tomorrow. Just because they aren't calling yet doesn't mean they won't, unless you cease talking to them. Nothing happens until there's motion. Marketing is your mover. It's your rainmaker. Stay the course, hold the faith, and keep stirring.

ARE YOU READY

to think like a marketer?

ARE YOU READY

to act like a marketer?

ARE YOU READY

to communicate like a marketer?

▪

You have all you need to make great things happen in your business right now.

You can do this.

You can stand out from the crowd, the clutter, and the competition.

You can make marketing easy, practical, and automatic.

All you have to do is start.

▪

START TODAY.

START RIGHT NOW.

Pick up that spoon and get stirring.

You'll be so glad you did.

Index

. ■ .

About the Author

L AURON SONNIER is a marketing advisor, speaker, and trainer. She leads Sonnier Marketing & Communications, Inc., which teaches aggressive companies how to stand out, stir the pot, and put marketing into action.

Lauron has dedicated her entire career to marketing in one form or another. She holds a BS degree in communications and has spent more than 20 years in the marketing trenches. She has worked in television, public relations, and advertising serving the needs of many. She has worked as a marketing director, championing a single cause. And, she's been a business owner herself relying on her own methods. Acutely aware of the issues facing small and large, new and mature businesses, Lauron teaches all how to integrate marketing into the day-to-day functions of their operation so marketing gets done and generates results. Simply put, she makes marketing practical, in both how it is understood and how it is implemented.

Lauron is a sought-out speaker and trainer for companies, organizations, and events throughout the United States and beyond. She packs a heavy serving of substance and energy into every presentation, exuding an obvious enthusiasm for her topic, her audience, and for teaching.

Lauron's expertise has been featured in media venues throughout the United States, including a series of interstitials on HoustonPBS called *Standing Out with Lauron Sonnier.* She is also author of *365 Ways to Stir the Pot and Put Marketing Into Action*, a daily marketing guide. Her growing suite of marketing tools and resources further emphasizes her love and dedication to helping entrepreneurs and growing businesses achieve marketing clarity, confidence, and success.

A Cajun from Louisiana, Lauron couldn't talk if you tied her hands. She lives outside of Houston, Texas, with her husband and two charming daughters.